Love and Relationships in Recovery: Building Connections Beyond Addiction

By Kaitlyn Doht

LOVE AND RELATIONSHIPS BUILDING RELATIONSHIPS BEYOND ADDICTION

First edition. October 27, 2024.

Copyright © 2024 Kaitlyn Doht.

ISBN: 979-8227741714

Written by Kaitlyn Doht.

"Recovery is not a single journey alone, but a path we walk together—where each step forward strengthens not only the self, but the love that sustains us."

Introduction: Love in a New Light

The purpose of Love and Relationships in Recovery: Building Connections Beyond Addiction is to guide individuals who are navigating the complex path of recovery while building or rebuilding relationships. Whether in romantic partnerships, family bonds, or friendships, relationships play a crucial role in sustaining long-term sobriety, providing support, and offering joy and connection beyond the confines of addiction. However, these relationships often face unique challenges and strains that require specific tools, self-awareness, and growth strategies. This book is intended to be a compassionate, practical, and realistic resource to help individuals in recovery understand, nurture, and maintain healthy relationships that support sobriety and mutual well-being.

When someone embarks on the journey of recovery, they're not only learning how to live without substance use but also relearning how to connect with others authentically. Recovery offers a fresh start, an opportunity to redefine old relationships, and to cultivate new ones that are healthy, fulfilling, and based on respect and honesty. Yet, this often involves confronting past hurts, overcoming fears, and addressing patterns that may have harmed relationships in the past. Love and Relationships in Recovery aims to help readers navigate these changes with empathy and actionable guidance.

The book acknowledges the varied nature of relationships in recovery. From repairing broken family bonds to developing meaningful friendships to entering new romantic partnerships, each relationship has unique needs and potential obstacles. By covering a range of topics — such as self-love, healthy communication, trust-building, boundaries, and spiritual connection — the book provides readers with essential tools for overcoming these challenges. Readers will also explore practical exercises to apply these concepts to their lives, fostering growth not just within relationships but also within themselves. This emphasis on practical tools is central to the book's purpose, equipping readers to take real, actionable steps toward healthier interactions and to develop self-sustaining habits that will support their relationships over time.

A unique aspect of this book is its focus on co-recovery, or supporting each other's healing journey in a way that respects each person's individuality while also strengthening the bond. It's written for individuals who seek to cultivate relationships where both partners or friends in recovery can share their experiences, support each other, and grow together without falling into patterns of co-dependency or enabling.

Love and Relationships in Recovery isn't a traditional recovery book focused solely on substance use or the journey of an individual; it's a relationship-centered approach that acknowledges the importance of human connection in healing. As readers progress through the book, they'll discover how relationships, when approached with understanding and healthy intentions, can be powerful allies in the path to lasting sobriety. For anyone who wants to create loving, supportive connections beyond addiction, this book offers a guide to building a life that's not only sober but full of genuine, nurturing relationships that contribute to a meaningful, balanced, and joyful life. Relationships hold a unique significance in recovery, as they provide essential support, encouragement, and emotional grounding. For individuals who have struggled with addiction, meaningful connections become a steady anchor, fostering a sense of purpose and helping them navigate both challenges and victories. Relationships go beyond simple companionship, offering the chance to reconnect with oneself and others through trust, honesty, and genuine compassion. These bonds are more than social support; they become a source of strength, helping people rediscover joy and stability lost during addiction.

Healthy relationships offer a supportive environment, creating a safe place to explore vulnerability, work through setbacks, and celebrate personal growth. Loved ones, friends, and family provide encouragement when the journey feels overwhelming, serving as a reminder of each person's goals and offering a sense of togetherness. Supportive relationships also bring accountability. Knowing there are people who care deeply can make all the difference during challenging times, reinforcing a commitment to sobriety.

Another reason relationships matter is the opportunity to repair past damage and nurture new, positive connections. Addiction often leads to broken trust, hurt feelings, and fractured bonds. Recovery allows for healing these wounds, building relationships that reflect healthier communication, respect, and trust. Apologizing, listening, and connecting openly with others are all part of this process. Recovery-focused relationships, especially those with people who understand the struggle firsthand, add an extra layer of empathy and shared understanding.

Relationships in recovery contribute to self-discovery, as building authentic bonds requires commitment to personal growth. Developing strong connections involves understanding one's own needs, setting boundaries, and learning open, honest communication. These skills not only benefit recovery but also lead to more fulfilling relationships. Self-awareness and a healthy sense of self-worth become the foundation of lasting, resilient connections.

Recovery relationships redefine love and connection, moving away from enabling behaviors or codependency. Many individuals with addiction histories have experienced relationships marked by unhealthy patterns, dependency, or imbalanced emotional support. Recovery offers a fresh start, where individuals learn the value of interdependent relationships that allow each person room for growth while maintaining mutual support.

Relationships in recovery remind individuals of their inherent worth and offer a source of joy, respect, and connection. These bonds go beyond self-healing, helping build a life that feels meaningful and enriching.

In recovery, relationships become both a source of joy and, at times, a unique set of challenges. Rebuilding trust and forming connections after addiction often feels daunting. The past may carry hurt, broken promises, and a sense of guilt or regret that lingers. Loved ones may struggle with lingering doubts, or uncertainty about how to support someone in recovery. These moments can be difficult, often requiring patience, humility, and a commitment to honest communication. A person may also face their own internal struggles, like fear of vulnerability or a tendency to withdraw when relationships become challenging.

Past behaviors shaped by addiction can make it hard to trust oneself in new or reestablished relationships. For some, there's an underlying fear of relapse or an impulse to avoid situations that may trigger unhealthy habits. Creating meaningful, healthy connections means working through these anxieties, taking risks with vulnerability, and resisting the urge to retreat when faced with emotional challenges. This work can feel exhausting at times, but it's essential for building relationships that are genuine and supportive.

An additional challenge lies in learning to set and respect boundaries. Before recovery, boundaries may have been either overly rigid or virtually nonexistent. Learning to find a balance, especially with loved ones or romantic partners, requires time and practice. Boundaries allow for healthier, more respectful connections where both individuals' needs are acknowledged. For someone in recovery, this can be unfamiliar territory, especially if past relationships were marked by codependency or lack of personal space. Establishing boundaries may initially feel uncomfortable, but it ultimately fosters respect, independence, and trust within the relationship.

There's also the reward of witnessing these connections deepen and flourish over time. Strong relationships offer a sense of accomplishment, as individuals realize they are capable of meaningful, healthy bonds. As communication improves and trust builds, relationships provide a place of belonging and understanding that reinforces one's commitment to sobriety. Partners, family, and friends may also grow alongside the individual in recovery, gaining their own insights and learning about the value of empathy, patience, and resilience.

In recovery, relationships create opportunities for growth that extend beyond one's own journey. Connecting with others allows people to reflect on their progress and celebrate milestones together. Simple acts of kindness, shared memories, and moments of mutual support help to shape a life that feels full and rewarding. Knowing there are people who genuinely care and celebrate each step toward healing builds confidence and self-worth.

Challenges continue to emerge throughout the process, but overcoming them brings a sense of empowerment. The strength required to build and maintain healthy relationships mirrors the strength needed to stay committed to recovery. As individuals confront and move past the barriers in their relationships, they become more resilient, learning how to navigate difficult situations without compromising their sobriety or sense of self.

In the end, the rewards of relationships in recovery far outweigh the challenges. Strong, healthy connections become a foundation that offers joy, encouragement, and unwavering support, forming a network of bonds that sustain and uplift, even through life's most difficult moments.

This book is designed as a practical guide to help individuals in recovery strengthen their relationships, navigate the complex dynamics of interpersonal connections, and build healthy support systems. Each chapter covers a specific aspect of relationships in recovery, offering insights, tools, and exercises that encourage growth, trust, and resilience in both romantic and non-romantic relationships. Throughout the book, readers will find suggestions, practical advice, and thought-provoking reflections meant to help them deepen connections and build a network of meaningful, supportive bonds that sustain them in sobriety.

Some readers may choose to follow the book chapter by chapter, while others may prefer to focus on topics that resonate most with their current needs or situations. The book is organized to allow for flexibility, making it easy to revisit chapters as relationships evolve or as new challenges arise. Each chapter includes reflective exercises designed to encourage self-awareness, provide space for honest communication, and foster healthier ways of connecting. By actively engaging with these exercises, readers can personalize the material, making it relevant to their unique experiences and growth in recovery.

In addition to reflection exercises, readers will find practical tools for managing relationship challenges, setting boundaries, and building trust. Whether working on personal growth or strengthening an existing relationship, these tools offer straightforward approaches that readers can apply immediately. The suggestions here are realistic and acknowledge that relationships in recovery require consistent effort and compassion. The exercises are intended to help readers not only reflect on their own needs but also consider the perspectives of loved ones, encouraging empathy and understanding as they work toward healthier relationships.

This book also encourages readers to revisit specific chapters or exercises whenever needed. Recovery is a lifelong journey, and relationships require attention, patience, and a commitment to growth. As relationships change and new challenges arise, the tools in this book can be revisited and adapted to fit each new stage. This flexibility allows readers to use the book not just as a one-time guide but as a lasting resource that can support them at various points along their recovery journey.

Beyond offering tools and exercises, this book serves as a reminder of the importance of connection, kindness, and shared growth. Each chapter reinforces the idea that relationships in recovery are about more than just companionship; they're about building a life filled with mutual respect, trust, and understanding. As readers work through the material, they'll find encouragement and inspiration to continue nurturing their relationships and deepening their connections, even when challenges emerge.

Above all, I hope this book serves you well, offering both guidance and support as you navigate the path of recovery in connection with those you care about. It's my wish that the insights, tools, and reflections here help you create relationships that are not only supportive but transformative, bringing you strength, encouragement, and joy as you move forward in sobriety. Let this book be a companion on your journey, one that offers perspective, compassion, and a reminder of the beauty of shared growth. Thank you for allowing me to be part of your recovery experience, and may your relationships be a source of lasting resilience and fulfillment.

Chapter 1: The Foundation of Self Love

Understanding the essence of self-love is fundamental for fostering healthy relationships. This vital concept creates a foundation where individuals can recognize their inherent worth, independent of external validation or the opinions of others. Embracing self-love allows for genuine connections with others, as it empowers individuals to engage without the burden of dependency or the fear of rejection. In the context of recovery, self-love becomes a powerful catalyst for change, enabling individuals to establish balanced, respectful interactions.

Engaging in self-acceptance lays the groundwork for nurturing relationships. Acknowledging both strengths and vulnerabilities promotes a compassionate view of oneself. This recognition is especially crucial for those in recovery, as past experiences may often evoke feelings of guilt or shame. A journey toward self-acceptance requires a deliberate choice to forgive oneself and embrace a holistic view of personal identity. By understanding that past actions do not diminish one's value, individuals can cultivate an authentic sense of self that contributes to healthier relational dynamics.

Respecting personal boundaries emerges as another key aspect of nurturing one's sense of worth. Boundaries protect emotional and physical well-being, creating a safe space for individuals to express themselves. Learning to communicate and uphold boundaries is essential for ensuring that relationships are equitable and reciprocal. Establishing clear limits fosters an environment where both partners can thrive, free from the fear of overstepping or being taken for granted. This respectful framework enhances communication, leading to deeper connections and shared understanding.

Personal growth enriches the journey of self-love, inviting individuals to explore their potential continually. Recovery often presents a unique opportunity for self-discovery, encouraging individuals to reflect on their values, passions, and aspirations. Embracing personal growth allows individuals to engage in continuous self-improvement, enhancing their ability to connect with others authentically. By prioritizing growth, individuals develop resilience, empathy, and maturity, qualities that significantly benefit relationships. This ongoing process empowers people to bring their best selves into every interaction, fostering deeper connections grounded in shared experiences and understanding.

Forgiveness plays a pivotal role in the practice of self-love, especially for those who have faced the challenges of addiction. Carrying the weight of past mistakes can create barriers to forming new, meaningful connections. Learning to forgive oneself involves recognizing the humanity in mistakes and understanding that they are part of the journey. By letting go of guilt and embracing self-compassion, individuals can open themselves to healthier relational dynamics. This act of forgiveness not only liberates the individual but also fosters a spirit of understanding and compassion toward others, creating a cycle of healing and growth.

Incorporating self-care into daily life is essential for nurturing a loving relationship with oneself. Prioritizing personal well-being manifests in various forms, from engaging in physical activity to pursuing hobbies that bring joy. This commitment to self-care not only replenishes emotional reserves but also communicates a message of worthiness. By taking time to nurture oneself, individuals cultivate resilience and stability, which translates into their interactions with others. Engaging in self-care practices creates an atmosphere where love can flourish, allowing individuals to give and receive affection without feeling depleted.

Confidence naturally arises from the practice of self-love. A strong sense of self-worth enables individuals to navigate relationships with assurance, reducing the need for external validation. Confidence manifests in many forms—assertiveness in expressing needs, clarity in setting boundaries, and the ability to engage in healthy conflict. When individuals approach relationships from a place of confidence, they contribute to a balanced partnership, where both parties feel valued and heard. This self-assuredness attracts like-minded individuals, fostering connections rooted in mutual respect and shared values.

Releasing the habit of comparison enhances the journey of self-love, allowing individuals to appreciate their unique journeys. Constantly measuring oneself against others can foster feelings of inadequacy, inhibiting personal growth and connection. Recognizing the individuality of each path encourages a mindset of appreciation rather than competition. By embracing authenticity, individuals attract relationships that celebrate their true selves. This authenticity fosters deeper connections, as partners engage from a place of genuine understanding and appreciation.

Inner peace is an outcome of cultivating self-love, creating a serene foundation for relationships. When individuals achieve a state of inner calm, they can engage with others in a more balanced, empathetic manner. This inner tranquility reduces reactivity, allowing for thoughtful responses to conflicts rather than impulsive reactions. The presence of inner peace contributes to a safe environment where both partners feel comfortable expressing themselves openly. This emotional stability fosters trust and deepens connections, creating a relational space filled with understanding and respect.

As individuals engage in self-love, they cultivate the qualities necessary for nurturing meaningful, supportive relationships. A strong sense of self-worth empowers them to seek connections that are healthy, balanced, and fulfilling. Approaching relationships with compassion and authenticity transforms interactions, allowing both individuals to grow together. Through the practice of self-love, individuals discover the beauty of genuine connections, rooted in mutual support and shared growth. The journey toward self-love is ongoing, and as individuals deepen their understanding of themselves, they inevitably enrich their relationships with others, paving the way for a more fulfilling and connected life.

Overcoming shame and guilt is an essential aspect of the journey toward healthy relationships in recovery. Many individuals face intense feelings of shame tied to their past behaviors, often rooted in their experiences with addiction. This internal struggle can create barriers to forming connections with others and can impact self-worth, making it challenging to engage fully in relationships. Acknowledging and addressing these emotions is crucial for healing and personal growth, allowing individuals to move forward with renewed strength and openness.

Shame often arises from a sense of unworthiness, leading individuals to believe they are inherently flawed or defective. This belief can stem from societal stigma surrounding addiction, past mistakes, and the often painful consequences of those actions. In recovery, it is vital to recognize that shame is a normal human emotion but does not have to define one's identity. Understanding that everyone has imperfections and experiences failures can help individuals reframe their narrative. Accepting that mistakes are part of the human experience allows for greater compassion toward oneself and others.

The process of overcoming guilt requires a similar reframing of perspective. Guilt often manifests as a feeling of responsibility for past actions that hurt others or oneself. While it can serve as a motivator for positive change, excessive guilt can lead to self-punishment and avoidance of relationships. Acknowledging guilt without becoming trapped by it is essential for personal growth. It is possible to learn from past mistakes, make amends where appropriate, and move forward with a renewed sense of purpose. This journey begins with self-forgiveness, recognizing that every person is capable of change and growth.

Engaging in open communication with trusted individuals can be a powerful tool for overcoming shame and guilt. Sharing personal experiences, including feelings of shame, can create a sense of relief and understanding. Vulnerability fosters connection, reminding individuals that they are not alone in their struggles. This process of sharing allows for empathy and support to flow both ways, reinforcing the idea that everyone is deserving of love and acceptance, regardless of their past. When individuals see that others can empathize with their journey, they often begin to lessen the weight of their shame and guilt. Building a supportive network is crucial in the recovery process, providing a space where individuals can express their feelings without fear of judgment. Engaging in group therapy or support groups creates opportunities to share experiences, fostering an environment of acceptance and healing. Hearing others' stories can help individuals realize that they are not defined by their past but by their commitment to change. This sense of community reinforces the understanding that recovery is a collective journey, where individuals uplift and encourage one another in their healing processes.

Practicing self-compassion is a powerful antidote to shame and guilt. This involves treating oneself with the same kindness and understanding that one would offer a friend. It means recognizing that everyone struggles and that making mistakes does not diminish one's worth. Developing self-compassion allows individuals to navigate their emotions without harsh judgment. It encourages them to acknowledge feelings of shame and guilt while choosing to respond with love and acceptance. This practice creates a nurturing internal dialogue that fosters resilience and personal growth.

Journaling can serve as a transformative tool in the process of overcoming shame and guilt. Writing down thoughts and feelings can help individuals clarify their emotions, identify triggers, and explore the root causes of their shame. This self-reflective practice provides an opportunity for catharsis, allowing individuals to confront and process their emotions. By putting feelings into words, they can gain perspective on their experiences and begin to shift their narratives toward healing and self-acceptance.

Engaging in mindfulness practices also plays a significant role in overcoming shame and guilt. Mindfulness encourages individuals to observe their thoughts and feelings without judgment, creating a sense of detachment from negative emotions. This practice allows individuals to acknowledge their feelings of shame or guilt while not letting them dictate their actions or self-worth. By cultivating mindfulness, individuals can develop a greater awareness of their emotional landscape, fostering acceptance and reducing the intensity of negative feelings.

Creating new, positive experiences can help individuals redefine their self-image. Engaging in activities that bring joy, fulfillment, and a sense of purpose can counterbalance feelings of shame and guilt. Pursuing hobbies, volunteering, or developing new skills allows individuals to connect with others and themselves in meaningful ways. These experiences create opportunities for positive reinforcement, enabling individuals to see their worth beyond past mistakes. This shift in perspective is vital for building healthy relationships, as it fosters confidence and a sense of belonging.

Seeking professional help, such as therapy or counseling, can provide invaluable support in overcoming shame and guilt. A trained professional can offer tools and strategies to address these emotions effectively. Therapy provides a safe space for individuals to explore their feelings, work through difficult experiences, and develop healthier coping mechanisms. Professional guidance can help individuals understand the impact of shame and guilt on their relationships and provide personalized strategies for moving forward.

Overcoming shame and guilt is not a linear journey but rather a continuous process that unfolds over time. It requires patience, self-compassion, and a willingness to engage with uncomfortable emotions. As individuals work through these feelings, they create space for healing and growth. This transformative journey fosters deeper connections, allowing them to approach relationships with openness, empathy, and a renewed sense of self-worth. Embracing the process of overcoming shame and guilt ultimately leads to more authentic and fulfilling relationships, enriching both individual lives and the connections they cultivate with others.

Building self-esteem in sobriety is a crucial aspect of recovery that significantly influences the quality of relationships individuals form. High self-esteem fosters confidence, encourages positive interactions, and enhances emotional resilience. For those recovering from addiction, rebuilding self-esteem can be particularly challenging due to the negative self-perceptions often ingrained by past experiences. Focusing on developing a strong sense of self-worth is essential for creating healthy, fulfilling connections.

Self-esteem is rooted in a deep understanding of personal value. In recovery, individuals must work to recognize and appreciate their inherent worth, regardless of past mistakes or the impact of addiction. Engaging in self-reflection can help uncover the core values and strengths that define one's identity. Identifying personal qualities, skills, and achievements, no matter how small, can create a foundation of self-worth. This practice encourages individuals to celebrate their progress in recovery, reinforcing the understanding that they are deserving of love and respect.

Setting achievable goals is another powerful strategy for building self-esteem. In sobriety, establishing small, realistic objectives provides a sense of accomplishment and fosters motivation. Each goal achieved contributes to a growing sense of confidence, allowing individuals to see their capabilities in action. Whether it's committing to a daily routine, participating in a new activity, or completing a project, these achievements cultivate self-efficacy and reinforce a positive self-image. As individuals recognize their ability to set and meet goals, they develop a belief in their potential, further enhancing their self-esteem. Surrounding oneself with positive influences is vital for fostering healthy self-esteem. The people with whom individuals choose to spend their time can significantly impact their self-perception. Building relationships with supportive, encouraging individuals creates an environment where self-worth can flourish. These positive influences provide affirmation, validation, and encouragement, reinforcing the belief that individuals are worthy of love and respect. Additionally, participating in support groups or recovery communities allows individuals to connect with others who understand their struggles, creating a sense of belonging that bolsters self-esteem.

Challenging negative self-talk is a critical component of building self-esteem. Many individuals recovering from addiction grapple with an inner critic that perpetuates feelings of inadequacy and unworthiness. Identifying these negative thoughts and replacing them with positive affirmations is essential for fostering a healthier self-image. Practicing self-compassion and recognizing that everyone has flaws and makes mistakes can help mitigate the impact of negative self-talk. Engaging in daily affirmations or writing down positive qualities can create a shift in mindset, encouraging individuals to view themselves through a more compassionate lens.

Engaging in activities that promote personal growth also contributes to building self-esteem in sobriety. Pursuing hobbies, developing new skills, or taking on challenges fosters a sense of accomplishment and fulfillment. These activities provide opportunities for self-discovery, allowing individuals to explore their interests and talents. Embracing new experiences can boost confidence and reinforce the understanding that they are capable of growth and change. Additionally, volunteering or helping others can provide a sense of purpose, further enhancing self-esteem through acts of kindness and service.

Practicing gratitude is a transformative tool for cultivating self-esteem in recovery. Regularly reflecting on positive aspects of life, no matter how small, fosters a mindset of appreciation and abundance. This practice encourages individuals to focus on their strengths, achievements, and the support they receive from others. By recognizing and celebrating the good in their lives, individuals can counterbalance feelings of inadequacy and build a more positive self-image. Gratitude can be expressed through journaling, verbal affirmations, or sharing experiences with others, reinforcing a sense of connection and fulfillment.

Establishing a routine can play a significant role in building self-esteem. Structure and consistency provide individuals with a sense of stability and purpose. Creating a daily routine that includes self-care practices, productive activities, and time for reflection fosters a sense of accomplishment and self-discipline. As individuals adhere to their routines, they experience a growing sense of control over their lives, reinforcing their self-worth. This newfound stability creates a fertile ground for healthy relationships to flourish, as individuals approach interactions with confidence and resilience.

Learning to accept compliments graciously is another essential aspect of building self-esteem. Many individuals in recovery struggle to accept positive feedback, often downplaying their achievements or attributing them to luck. Practicing the acceptance of compliments can help individuals internalize the positive reinforcement they receive from others. This practice involves acknowledging the compliment, expressing gratitude, and allowing oneself to truly believe in the recognition. By accepting praise, individuals reinforce their sense of worth and create a positive feedback loop that enhances self-esteem.

Confronting past traumas is a vital part of building self-esteem in sobriety. Many individuals carry the weight of unresolved emotional pain that can hinder their self-worth. Engaging in therapy or counseling provides a safe space to process these experiences and develop coping strategies. Addressing past traumas allows individuals to release the burdens of shame and guilt, fostering a healthier self-image. As they work through these emotions, individuals can cultivate a sense of empowerment, reinforcing the understanding that they are not defined by their past.

Building self-esteem in sobriety is a multifaceted journey that requires patience, self-compassion, and commitment. As individuals engage in practices that promote self-acceptance, set achievable goals, and surround themselves with positive influences, they cultivate a deeper understanding of their inherent worth. This growing self-esteem not only enhances personal well-being but also enriches relationships, allowing individuals to connect with others from a place of confidence and authenticity. The journey toward building self-esteem is an ongoing process, one that opens the door to deeper, more meaningful connections with others and within oneself.

In embracing the principles of self-worth, individuals pave the way for healthier relationships, free from the shadows of shame and guilt. The process of building self-esteem is empowering, reminding individuals that they are deserving of love, respect, and happiness. Through this journey, they learn to embrace their true selves, creating a solid foundation for connections that are not only supportive but also deeply fulfilling.

Engaging in practical exercises is essential for building self-esteem and fostering healthy relationships in recovery. These activities not only provide individuals with tangible steps to enhance their self-worth but also create opportunities for self-discovery and personal growth. By incorporating affirmations, self-reflection practices, and mindfulness techniques into daily routines, individuals can cultivate a deeper sense of self-love and acceptance.

Affirmations serve as powerful tools for reshaping negative thought patterns and reinforcing positive self-beliefs. These positive statements encourage individuals to challenge their inner critic and embrace a more compassionate view of themselves. To create effective affirmations, individuals should focus on specific qualities or attributes they want to nurture. For instance, affirmations like "I am worthy of love and respect" or "I am capable of achieving my goals" can help individuals internalize these beliefs. Writing these affirmations down and placing them in visible areas, such as mirrors or workspaces, reinforces their importance and encourages daily practice. Reciting affirmations aloud or in front of a mirror can also enhance their impact, allowing individuals to connect with the words on a deeper level.

Incorporating affirmations into a morning routine sets a positive tone for the day. Taking a few moments each morning to read or recite affirmations can create a mindset of empowerment and resilience. Additionally, individuals can experiment with different affirmations that resonate with them, adapting their statements as they grow and evolve in recovery. By consistently practicing affirmations, individuals gradually shift their internal dialogue, fostering a greater sense of self-acceptance and confidence.

Self-reflection practices play a pivotal role in understanding personal values, strengths, and areas for growth. Journaling is an effective method for engaging in self-reflection, allowing individuals to articulate their thoughts and feelings on paper. Setting aside dedicated time each day or week to journal can create a structured space for introspection. Prompts such as "What am I proud of today?" or "What challenges did I face, and how did I overcome them?" encourage individuals to explore their experiences and emotions. Writing about accomplishments, no matter how small, reinforces a sense of achievement and fosters a positive self-image.

Gratitude journaling is another valuable practice for cultivating self-esteem. Regularly reflecting on the aspects of life for which individuals are grateful shifts the focus from negative experiences to positive ones. Listing three to five things each day that evoke feelings of gratitude fosters an appreciation for life's blessings, no matter how insignificant they may seem. This practice not only enhances self-esteem but also encourages a mindset of abundance and positivity. Creating a self-reflection routine can also involve identifying personal values and goals. Individuals can take time to contemplate what is truly important to them and what they aspire to achieve. Writing down core values, such as honesty, compassion, or creativity, can provide clarity and direction in decision-making. Establishing specific, achievable goals aligned with these values fosters a sense of purpose and self-worth. Regularly reviewing and adjusting these goals allows individuals to track their progress and celebrate their achievements, further reinforcing positive self-perceptions.

Mindfulness techniques are powerful practices for enhancing self-awareness and fostering emotional regulation. Mindfulness encourages individuals to stay present in the moment, reducing anxiety about the past or future. One effective mindfulness practice is deep breathing exercises. Taking a few minutes each day to focus on breath can create a sense of calm and clarity. Individuals can find a quiet space, close their eyes, and take slow, deep breaths, allowing themselves to feel grounded and centered. This practice can also be integrated into moments of stress or anxiety, providing a quick way to regain composure.

Mindful meditation is another technique that can significantly enhance self-esteem. Setting aside time for meditation allows individuals to connect with their thoughts and feelings without judgment. Various guided meditation apps or resources can help individuals find practices that resonate with them. Meditating on self-acceptance, compassion, and love creates a nurturing environment for personal growth. Over time, individuals can cultivate a greater sense of self-awareness and compassion through consistent meditation practices.

Engaging in mindful movement, such as yoga or tai chi, can also promote self-acceptance and body positivity. These practices encourage individuals to tune into their bodies and honor their physical sensations. Focusing on movement and breath fosters a deeper connection with oneself, allowing individuals to appreciate their bodies for what they can do rather than how they appear. Establishing a regular practice of mindful movement can create a positive relationship with one's body, enhancing self-esteem and overall well-being.

Connecting with nature is another way to practice mindfulness and self-reflection. Spending time outdoors fosters a sense of peace and connection to the world around us. Engaging in activities such as hiking, walking, or simply sitting in a park allows individuals to observe their surroundings and find solace in nature. This practice encourages individuals to be present, appreciate the beauty of their environment, and reflect on their emotions in a serene setting.

Creating a vision board can serve as a creative self-reflection exercise that enhances self-esteem. Vision boards are visual representations of personal goals, aspirations, and values. Individuals can gather images, quotes, and symbols that resonate with their desired future and arrange them on a board. This tangible representation of dreams and aspirations serves as a daily reminder of personal worth and potential. Displaying the vision board in a visible area reinforces motivation and inspires individuals to pursue their goals.

Lastly, seeking feedback from trusted friends or mentors can provide valuable insights into one's strengths and areas for growth. Engaging in open conversations about self-perception can foster a greater understanding of how others view us. This practice can help individuals recognize positive qualities they may overlook, reinforcing a more balanced self-image. Constructive feedback encourages personal growth and self-improvement, contributing to building self-esteem.

Incorporating these practical exercises into daily life creates a holistic approach to building self-esteem and fostering healthy relationships. Engaging in affirmations, self-reflection, mindfulness, and creative expression allows individuals to cultivate a deeper sense of self-worth and acceptance. As they commit to these practices, individuals empower themselves to embrace their true selves, paving the way for more meaningful connections with others.

Through consistent effort and dedication, the journey toward building self-esteem becomes an enriching experience, leading to personal growth, resilience, and authentic relationships. Embracing the transformative power of self-love and self-acceptance lays a solid foundation for a fulfilling life in recovery. As individuals cultivate these practices, they open themselves to the beauty of connection, love, and the possibility of healthier, more fulfilling relationships.

As chapter one concludes, it becomes clear that cultivating self-love is not just an individual endeavor but a communal one, influencing every relationship an individual engages in. The journey toward self-acceptance and love is filled with challenges and rewards, each step providing valuable lessons that contribute to personal growth. Embracing this foundation sets the stage for the subsequent chapters, where the exploration of love, relationships, and connection in recovery will continue. Each chapter will build upon the insights gained from understanding self-love, emphasizing its role in fostering healthier interactions and deeper bonds with others. The journey ahead is one of exploration and discovery, inviting individuals to embrace the beauty of love, both for themselves and for those around them.

Chapter 2: Relearning Healthy Communication

Healthy communication forms the backbone of successful relationships, particularly during recovery. The ability to express thoughts, feelings, and needs effectively enhances understanding between partners. In the context of recovery, where emotions can often be heightened, clear communication becomes a necessity. When individuals are transparent with each other, they create an environment of trust and safety that is crucial for emotional intimacy.

Addiction often leads to a breakdown in communication patterns. Relationships can be fraught with miscommunication, defensiveness, and emotional distance. Recovery offers the opportunity to rebuild these foundations. Engaging in open dialogue about feelings, past experiences, and expectations helps mend the fractures caused by addiction. This rebuilding process requires effort and dedication but ultimately lays the groundwork for healthier interactions.

Active listening is a critical component of effective communication. This skill involves fully engaging with a partner's words and emotions. It requires presence, attention, and a genuine willingness to understand. When both individuals practice active listening, they not only validate each other's experiences but also create space for vulnerability. This deeper connection fosters emotional support and strengthens the bond between partners.

Expressing needs openly is vital in recovery relationships. Individuals often grapple with their own challenges and may struggle to articulate what they require from their partner. By clearly stating their needs, partners can provide each other with the necessary support to navigate the difficulties of recovery. This practice encourages interdependence, promoting a sense of partnership and teamwork that is essential in overcoming challenges together.

Conflict is an inevitable part of any relationship. However, how couples manage conflict is what defines the strength of their bond. Constructive conflict resolution relies heavily on communication skills. Instead of resorting to avoidance or aggression, couples can engage in discussions that honor each other's perspectives. This approach allows both partners to feel heard and respected, reducing the likelihood of resentment.

Setting boundaries is another crucial aspect of communication in recovery. Healthy relationships require clear limits to protect emotional well-being and maintain sobriety. Communicating boundaries assertively helps both partners understand each other's limits and fosters mutual respect. When boundaries are established, individuals can navigate their relationship with clarity, reducing the risk of misunderstandings and violations.

Building self-awareness enhances communication. Understanding personal triggers, emotions, and communication styles allows individuals to engage with their partner more effectively. Self-awareness enables individuals to express themselves without projecting past hurts onto their partner. This level of reflection contributes to healthier interactions and reduces unnecessary conflict.

Vulnerability plays a significant role in fostering intimacy through communication. Sharing fears, insecurities, and hopes can deepen connections between partners. When individuals feel safe to express their vulnerabilities, it opens the door for genuine understanding and support. This shared vulnerability nurtures a climate of trust, reinforcing the relationship's foundation.

Practicing empathy enhances communication. The ability to see a situation from a partner's perspective allows for compassion and understanding. Empathy encourages patience and reduces defensiveness during challenging conversations. When both partners approach discussions with empathy, they cultivate a supportive environment conducive to growth and healing.

The impact of past experiences cannot be understated in recovery. Individuals may carry emotional baggage from previous relationships that influences their current interactions. Recognizing and addressing these influences is essential for effective communication. By acknowledging past patterns and consciously choosing healthier approaches, individuals can break the cycle of destructive communication.

In recovery, individuals may encounter feelings of shame and guilt that complicate communication. These emotions can lead to withdrawal or defensiveness, creating barriers to honest dialogue. Learning to discuss these feelings openly can facilitate healing. By addressing shame and guilt within a supportive framework, couples can work together to navigate these challenging emotions, fostering a deeper connection.

Engaging in structured communication exercises can enhance skills. Practicing role-playing scenarios or utilizing communication techniques in a supportive setting helps individuals refine their abilities. By consciously focusing on their communication style, individuals can become more effective partners in their relationships.

Continuous improvement in communication is key. Recovery is a journey of growth, and the skills necessary for healthy communication can always be refined. Embracing this mindset encourages individuals to be open to feedback and learning, promoting ongoing development in their relationships.

In the realm of recovery, effective communication is not just beneficial; it is essential. The ability to communicate openly and honestly fosters deeper emotional connections, reduces conflicts, and promotes healthy interactions. As individuals commit to developing these skills, they create a nurturing environment that supports their recovery journey and strengthens their relationships. The practice of healthy communication will serve as a guiding principle throughout this journey, enhancing the quality of connections and paving the way for lasting bonds.

Defensive communication often arises from fear, insecurity, and past experiences. Individuals in recovery may have developed these defensive mechanisms as a way to protect themselves from hurt or rejection. This type of communication can create barriers in relationships, preventing genuine connection and understanding. Recognizing the patterns of defensiveness is the first step toward fostering more open and honest communication.

When one partner feels threatened or criticized, the instinct may be to respond with defensiveness. This reaction often escalates conflicts, causing partners to become entrenched in their positions rather than seeking resolution. Shifting from a defensive mindset to one of openness requires intentional effort and self-awareness. Acknowledging one's triggers and emotional responses can help individuals recognize when they are falling into defensive patterns.

Open communication thrives on vulnerability and honesty. Creating an environment where both partners feel safe to express themselves is crucial. This safety allows individuals to share their thoughts and feelings without the fear of judgment. Engaging in conversations that invite vulnerability fosters emotional intimacy and strengthens the relationship's foundation. Partners can practice sharing their feelings, needs, and concerns in a way that promotes understanding rather than defensiveness.

Practicing nonverbal communication enhances openness. Body language, facial expressions, and tone of voice all play significant roles in conveying messages. When partners communicate with openness, their nonverbal cues should align with their words. Maintaining eye contact, adopting a relaxed posture, and using a calm tone can help create a more welcoming atmosphere for dialogue. This alignment reassures partners that their intentions are sincere and that they are genuinely interested in understanding each other.

Active listening becomes even more essential when striving for open communication. Listening without interruption or judgment creates a space where partners can share their thoughts freely. Demonstrating that you are fully engaged in what the other person is saying fosters trust. Reflecting back what has been heard shows understanding and encourages the speaker to elaborate on their feelings. This practice not only promotes clarity but also validates the speaker's emotions.

When navigating sensitive topics, the use of "I" statements can transform defensive communication into open dialogue. Instead of saying "You never listen to me," expressing feelings through "I" statements can significantly alter the conversation's tone. For instance, "I feel unheard when you don't respond to my concerns" shifts the focus from blame to personal experience. This approach reduces defensiveness and invites a more constructive conversation, as it encourages partners to respond to feelings rather than feeling attacked. Developing a shared vocabulary for discussing feelings can further enhance communication. Agreeing on specific terms to express emotions can reduce misunderstandings. For example, instead of using vague language, partners can articulate their feelings with precise words like "frustrated," "anxious," or "overwhelmed." This clarity allows for deeper discussions and helps partners respond more effectively to each other's needs.

Practicing patience is essential when moving from defensive to open communication. Old habits are challenging to break, and it may take time to establish new patterns. Recognizing that slip-ups may occur and being gentle with oneself and one's partner is vital. Celebrating small successes in communication can reinforce positive behavior and encourage ongoing growth.

Seeking professional support can be beneficial in this transition. Couples therapy or communication workshops provide a safe space to explore and develop effective communication strategies. A trained facilitator can guide partners through exercises that promote vulnerability and understanding, helping to establish a foundation of open communication. This external support can be invaluable in navigating complex emotional landscapes and learning new skills.

Cultivating empathy enhances the journey from defensiveness to openness. Understanding the emotional struggles of oneself and one's partner fosters compassion. Practicing empathy involves putting oneself in the other's shoes and recognizing their feelings as valid. When partners approach conversations with empathy, they create an environment conducive to healing and growth.

Embracing a mindset of curiosity rather than judgment promotes open communication. Asking open-ended questions encourages partners to explore their thoughts and feelings more deeply. Instead of making assumptions or jumping to conclusions, partners can foster a dialogue that leads to greater understanding. This curiosity allows both individuals to feel valued and appreciated, deepening their emotional connection.

Taking breaks during heated discussions can help prevent defensiveness from taking over. If emotions run high, pausing the conversation allows both partners to cool down and reflect. This break can lead to more productive discussions later, where both individuals can express their thoughts without the interference of heightened emotions. Resuming the conversation with a calmer mindset creates a more constructive atmosphere for open dialogue.

The journey from defensive to open communication is a continual process. As individuals evolve in their recovery and their relationships, the ability to communicate openly can significantly impact their connection. Commitment to this growth requires patience, self-awareness, and practice. As partners work together to foster open communication, they create a stronger foundation for their relationship, enhancing their emotional intimacy and mutual understanding.

Every step taken toward open communication is a step away from the barriers that defensiveness creates. Embracing vulnerability, active listening, and empathy transforms the way partners interact. This shift not only enriches their relationship but also serves as a model for healthy communication in all areas of life. The commitment to move away from defensiveness cultivates a nurturing environment, fostering growth, connection, and love in the journey of recovery.

Listening skills and empathy development are critical components of effective communication in recovery relationships. These elements create a strong foundation for understanding and connecting with partners on a deeper emotional level. Cultivating these skills enhances the overall quality of communication, promoting trust and intimacy. Individuals often underestimate the power of listening and empathy in fostering healthy relationships. Learning to listen actively and empathize with a partner's experiences can transform interactions and strengthen the bond between partners.

Active listening involves fully engaging with the speaker, focusing on their words, emotions, and body language. It requires setting aside distractions and giving the speaker your undivided attention. This practice signals to the speaker that their thoughts and feelings are valued. By listening intently, individuals create a safe space for their partner to express themselves openly. Acknowledging feelings and validating experiences through active listening fosters a deeper emotional connection. This practice encourages partners to share their vulnerabilities, building a foundation of trust and intimacy.

Empathy goes hand in hand with active listening. It involves understanding and sharing the feelings of another person. Cultivating empathy requires individuals to step outside of their own experiences and genuinely consider what their partner is feeling. This emotional attunement strengthens relationships and fosters a sense of connection. Empathy allows partners to respond to each other with compassion and understanding, reducing misunderstandings and conflict.

One powerful way to develop listening skills is through reflective listening. This technique involves paraphrasing what the speaker has said to ensure comprehension. Reflective listening not only shows the speaker that they have been heard but also provides an opportunity to clarify any misunderstandings. When partners engage in reflective listening, they create a dialogue that promotes deeper understanding and connection.

Nonverbal cues play a significant role in effective listening. Body language, facial expressions, and eye contact convey messages beyond words. Maintaining open and inviting body language, such as leaning slightly forward or nodding, indicates attentiveness. Eye contact reinforces the connection and demonstrates genuine interest in what the speaker is saying. Being mindful of nonverbal signals enhances the effectiveness of communication, creating a more supportive atmosphere for dialogue.

Empathy can be cultivated through various practices. One effective exercise is to put oneself in the partner's shoes. Imagining how they might feel in a specific situation allows for greater understanding and compassion. This practice encourages individuals to consider their partner's perspective, fostering emotional connection. Engaging in empathy-building exercises, such as journaling about experiences from the partner's viewpoint, can further enhance understanding.

Another powerful tool for developing empathy is storytelling. Sharing personal experiences allows partners to connect on a deeper emotional level. When individuals recount their stories, they invite their partners to understand their feelings and struggles. This sharing not only fosters empathy but also creates a sense of solidarity, reminding partners that they are not alone in their journeys.

Practicing patience is essential in the development of listening skills and empathy. It is natural for individuals to want to respond quickly, but taking a moment to pause and reflect before speaking can lead to more thoughtful responses. Patience allows partners to fully absorb what is being said and consider the best way to respond. This mindfulness enhances the overall quality of communication, creating a space for deeper understanding.

Feedback plays a critical role in developing listening and empathy skills. Encouraging partners to provide feedback on each other's communication styles fosters growth. Constructive feedback helps individuals recognize areas for improvement and reinforces positive behaviors. This process creates an environment where both partners feel supported in their efforts to enhance their communication skills.

Engaging in group activities can also promote the development of listening skills and empathy. Participating in group discussions, workshops, or support groups provides opportunities to practice these skills in a supportive environment. Listening to others' experiences and perspectives expands understanding and encourages individuals to consider viewpoints outside their own. These interactions foster a sense of community and connection, reinforcing the importance of empathy in relationships.

Self-reflection is a vital component of developing listening skills and empathy. Taking time to examine one's own emotions, triggers, and communication patterns can lead to greater self-awareness. Understanding how past experiences may influence current interactions enables individuals to approach conversations with a more open mindset. This self-awareness enhances the ability to listen actively and respond with empathy.

Creating rituals for open communication can enhance listening skills and empathy development. Setting aside dedicated time to check in with each other fosters an environment of trust and connection. During these moments, partners can share their thoughts and feelings without distractions. Engaging in this regular practice strengthens the emotional bond and reinforces the importance of active listening and empathy.

Embracing vulnerability enhances the development of these skills. Sharing fears, insecurities, and hopes invites partners to engage more deeply with one another. This openness encourages empathy and fosters a climate of understanding. When individuals feel safe to express their vulnerabilities, they create a space for their partner to do the same, strengthening their emotional connection.

Recognizing the value of silence can be a powerful aspect of listening and empathy. Silence allows space for reflection and processing. During conversations, moments of silence can encourage individuals to think deeply about what has been shared. This pause enhances understanding and provides an opportunity for more thoughtful responses.

The journey toward developing effective listening skills and empathy is ongoing. It requires commitment, practice, and a willingness to grow. As individuals embrace these skills, they cultivate stronger connections and healthier relationships. The ability to listen actively and respond with empathy transforms interactions, paving the way for deeper emotional bonds and greater understanding.

In recovery relationships, the importance of listening and empathy cannot be overstated. These skills enhance communication, promote emotional intimacy, and foster resilience. By prioritizing active listening and empathy, partners can navigate the complexities of recovery together, creating a foundation for lasting love and connection. Embracing these practices allows individuals to support one another through the ups and downs of recovery, reinforcing the idea that they are not alone in their journeys.

Practical tools for enhancing communication skills in recovery relationships are essential for fostering understanding and resolving conflicts. These tools provide individuals with strategies to navigate difficult conversations and promote healthy interactions. Implementing effective conflict resolution techniques, along with engaging in active listening exercises, equips partners with the skills necessary to communicate openly and constructively.

Conflict resolution is a vital component of healthy relationships, particularly in recovery, where emotions can run high and past traumas may surface. The ability to address disagreements constructively can strengthen the bond between partners and create a safe space for vulnerability. Effective conflict resolution involves several key steps that partners can practice together.

The first step in resolving conflict is to create a safe environment for discussion. Setting the stage for open communication requires both partners to approach the conversation with respect and a willingness to listen. Establishing ground rules for the discussion can help create this safe space. Ground rules might include allowing each person to speak without interruption, using "I" statements to express feelings, and focusing on the issue at hand rather than personal attacks.

Active listening is a crucial aspect of conflict resolution. When partners actively listen to each other, they validate each other's feelings and experiences. This validation fosters understanding and creates an atmosphere of respect. To practice active listening during conflicts, partners can employ reflective listening techniques. Paraphrasing what the other person has said and reflecting back their emotions helps ensure that both parties feel heard and understood.

An important tool in conflict resolution is the use of "I" statements. These statements help express feelings and needs without placing blame on the other person. For example, saying "I feel hurt when you don't acknowledge my efforts" instead of "You never appreciate what I do" focuses on personal feelings rather than accusing the partner. This approach encourages open dialogue and reduces defensiveness, allowing for a more productive conversation.

Identifying the underlying needs and interests of both partners is another critical step in conflict resolution. Often, conflicts arise from unmet needs or differing expectations. By discussing these needs openly, partners can work together to find mutually beneficial solutions. This approach shifts the focus from the disagreement itself to understanding what each partner requires to feel heard and valued.

Taking breaks during intense discussions can also be an effective strategy. When emotions escalate, it can be helpful to pause the conversation and agree to revisit it later. This break allows both partners to cool down and gather their thoughts, reducing the likelihood of escalating tensions. After the break, partners can reengage in the conversation with a clearer mindset and a renewed commitment to understanding each other.

In addition to conflict resolution techniques, engaging in active listening exercises can enhance communication skills in recovery relationships. These exercises provide opportunities for partners to practice their listening skills and deepen their emotional connection. One effective exercise is the "listening circle." In this activity, partners take turns speaking while the other listens attentively. The listener refrains from interrupting or responding until the speaker has finished. This practice fosters active listening and reinforces the importance of being fully present during conversations.

Another valuable exercise is the "empathy mapping" technique. In this activity, partners identify a specific situation where they felt misunderstood or hurt. Each partner takes turns sharing their perspective while the other listens without interrupting. Afterward, the listener reflects on what they heard and expresses empathy for the speaker's feelings. This exercise enhances understanding and strengthens the emotional bond between partners.

Creating a communication journal can also be a helpful tool for recovery relationships. In this journal, partners can write down their thoughts, feelings, and experiences related to communication. This practice encourages self-reflection and provides a space for individuals to articulate their emotions. Reviewing the journal together can facilitate discussions about areas for improvement and celebrate progress in communication skills.

Role-playing can serve as a practical exercise for honing conflict resolution and communication skills. Partners can take on different scenarios or past conflicts and practice how they would approach the situation differently. This exercise provides an opportunity to experiment with new techniques, such as using "I" statements or active listening, in a safe and supportive environment. Role-playing allows partners to gain insight into each other's perspectives and reinforces the importance of empathy.

Integrating mindfulness practices into communication can also enhance the effectiveness of interactions. Mindfulness encourages individuals to be present in the moment, reducing distractions and enhancing focus during conversations. Partners can practice mindfulness techniques, such as deep breathing or grounding exercises, before engaging in difficult discussions. This approach promotes emotional regulation and fosters a calm atmosphere for open communication.

Establishing regular check-ins can be a powerful tool for maintaining healthy communication in recovery relationships. Setting aside dedicated time to discuss feelings, concerns, and experiences fosters ongoing dialogue. During these check-ins, partners can share what is working well in their relationship and identify any areas that may require attention. This practice encourages proactive communication and strengthens the emotional connection between partners.

Creating a shared vocabulary can also enhance communication in recovery relationships. Partners can develop a set of phrases or words that resonate with both individuals, allowing for more effective expression of feelings and needs. This shared language provides a foundation for understanding and ensures that both partners are on the same page when discussing sensitive topics.

Practicing gratitude is another valuable tool for enhancing communication in recovery relationships. Taking time to express appreciation for one another fosters a positive atmosphere and reinforces the emotional bond. Partners can incorporate gratitude practices into their daily routines, such as sharing what they appreciate about each other during mealtime or before bed. This simple yet powerful practice promotes connection and reminds partners of the positive aspects of their relationship.

Establishing boundaries is essential in maintaining healthy communication in recovery relationships. Partners must communicate their needs and limits openly, ensuring that both individuals feel respected and valued. Discussing boundaries helps prevent misunderstandings and creates a safe environment for open dialogue.

Regularly revisiting communication goals can enhance the effectiveness of these practical tools. Partners can assess their progress in developing listening skills and conflict resolution techniques, celebrating successes and identifying areas for growth. This ongoing commitment to improvement fosters a culture of open communication and reinforces the importance of continuous learning in relationships.

As partners integrate these practical tools into their communication practices, they will strengthen their relationship and enhance their ability to navigate challenges together. The journey toward improved communication requires dedication and effort, but the rewards are profound. Enhanced understanding, emotional intimacy, and resilience in the face of adversity will ultimately foster a loving and supportive environment where both partners can thrive in their recovery journey.

Effective communication is the cornerstone of healthy relationships, especially in the context of recovery. By embracing the principles and practical tools discussed throughout this chapter, partners can navigate the complexities of their emotional landscapes and cultivate deeper connections. The journey toward improved communication involves ongoing practice and dedication, yet the rewards are invaluable. A relationship built on open dialogue, empathy, and understanding not only strengthens the bond between partners but also supports individual growth in recovery. As couples continue to develop their communication skills, they create a safe haven where love can flourish, resilience can grow, and both partners can heal together.

Chapter 3: Rebuilding Trust After Addiction

Understanding the impact of addiction on trust is crucial for rebuilding relationships in recovery. Addiction often creates a landscape of broken promises, betrayal, and emotional distance. Trust, once shattered, requires intentional effort and commitment to repair. The experience of addiction affects not only the individual struggling with substance use but also the loved ones who are left to navigate the aftermath. The journey to restore trust involves acknowledging the wounds caused by addiction and actively working toward healing.

Addiction can distort perceptions and alter behaviors. Many individuals struggling with substance use may prioritize their addiction over relationships, leading to neglect and emotional harm. This disregard can erode the trust built over time. Partners may feel abandoned, confused, or betrayed, grappling with the reality that their loved one is not fully present. Rebuilding trust requires recognizing how addiction has shaped both partners' experiences and acknowledging the pain it has caused.

Betrayal is a powerful force that can linger long after the addiction is addressed. A partner may feel deceived by the lies and manipulations that often accompany substance use. These feelings of betrayal can manifest as anger, resentment, and hurt, making it difficult to rebuild trust. Recognizing and validating these emotions is a necessary step in the healing process. Both partners must understand that trust can be rebuilt, but it requires time, patience, and consistent effort.

The journey of recovery is often filled with ups and downs, creating an emotional rollercoaster for both individuals involved. The individual in recovery may struggle with feelings of guilt and shame for the harm caused to their partner. Simultaneously, the partner may battle their own feelings of insecurity and doubt regarding their loved one's commitment to change. Both partners must navigate these emotions with care, recognizing that rebuilding trust is a collaborative effort.

Establishing open lines of communication is vital in rebuilding trust. Both partners must feel safe expressing their thoughts and feelings without fear of judgment or retribution. Honest conversations about the impact of addiction on their relationship can create a foundation for healing. This dialogue may include discussing past hurts, exploring triggers, and identifying how both partners can support each other moving forward.

Creating a shared vision for the future can also aid in rebuilding trust. Partners can work together to establish goals that promote mutual growth and healing. This shared vision provides a sense of direction and purpose, reinforcing the commitment to rebuild trust. It allows both partners to invest in the relationship, fostering a sense of teamwork as they navigate their recovery journeys.

Consistency is key in rebuilding trust. Actions must align with words for trust to be restored. The individual in recovery must demonstrate reliability and accountability, showing their partner that they are committed to change. This consistency may involve making and keeping promises, attending support meetings, and engaging in healthy coping strategies. Over time, these consistent actions can help rebuild the trust that was lost.

As trust is rebuilt, it is essential to recognize that setbacks may occur. The road to recovery is not linear, and challenges will arise. Both partners must approach these setbacks with understanding and compassion. When trust is tested, open communication can help navigate the situation and prevent further damage. The ability to discuss challenges openly can strengthen the relationship and reinforce the commitment to rebuild trust.

Forgiveness plays a significant role in the rebuilding process. Both partners must be willing to let go of past hurts to move forward. This does not mean forgetting or condoning the behavior but rather acknowledging the pain and choosing to work toward healing. Forgiveness is a journey that requires effort from both partners and can take time. It is essential to approach forgiveness with an open heart and a willingness to understand each other's experiences.

Engaging in therapy or support groups can provide a safe space for both partners to process their emotions and work through the challenges of rebuilding trust. Professional guidance can help facilitate difficult conversations and provide tools for effective communication. Additionally, support groups can connect partners with others who have experienced similar struggles, fostering a sense of community and understanding.

Rebuilding trust after addiction is a profound journey that requires dedication and resilience. Both partners must be committed to the process and understand that trust is earned over time. By acknowledging the impact of addiction on their relationship and actively working toward healing, couples can emerge stronger and more connected.

Restoring trust is not just about overcoming past hurts but also about creating a new foundation built on mutual respect and understanding. As both partners invest in their recovery and the relationship, they can cultivate a deeper bond that is rooted in authenticity and love.

The emotional work involved in rebuilding trust can be challenging but ultimately rewarding. The journey fosters personal growth, self-awareness, and a renewed appreciation for the relationship. As trust is rebuilt, partners can experience a renewed sense of connection, intimacy, and commitment, paving the way for a healthier future together.

Regaining trust with loved ones after addiction is a process that requires intentionality, vulnerability, and consistent effort. Each step taken towards restoring trust brings partners closer to healing. This journey involves both understanding the impact of past behaviors and actively engaging in new practices that foster trust.

The first step in this process is acknowledging the hurt caused by addiction. An individual in recovery must recognize how their actions have affected their partner and others. This acknowledgment requires honesty and humility, as it may bring up feelings of guilt and shame. Validating the emotions of loved ones is essential. A simple acknowledgment of their pain can lay the groundwork for deeper conversations about the future.

Taking responsibility is another vital step. Accepting accountability for past actions demonstrates a commitment to change. This involves recognizing the specific behaviors that led to the breakdown of trust and expressing genuine remorse. Offering a heartfelt apology can be incredibly powerful, but it must be accompanied by actions that reflect a desire to make amends. Actions speak louder than words; therefore, a commitment to change must manifest through consistent behavior.

Open communication plays a crucial role in regaining trust. Establishing a safe space for honest dialogue allows both partners to express their feelings, fears, and hopes without judgment. Active listening is key during these conversations. Partners should practice reflecting back what they hear to ensure understanding. This practice not only fosters clarity but also deepens emotional connection. By sharing vulnerabilities, both partners can create a stronger bond built on empathy and understanding.

Setting boundaries can help re-establish trust. Clearly defined boundaries create a sense of safety for both partners. The individual in recovery should discuss their needs and limitations while inviting their partner to share theirs. Boundaries might involve discussions about triggers, expectations for social interactions, or communication preferences. By creating mutual agreements, both partners can feel more secure and supported in their relationship.

Demonstrating consistent behavior is vital in rebuilding trust. The individual in recovery must follow through on commitments and promises, no matter how small. Consistency builds reliability, showing that they can be counted on. This might involve attending support meetings regularly, being open about their recovery journey, or maintaining honesty in everyday interactions. Each positive action reinforces the message that they are committed to rebuilding trust.

Another significant aspect of regaining trust involves transparency. Openness about feelings, struggles, and progress in recovery fosters a sense of partnership. The individual in recovery should feel empowered to share their journey, including challenges they may face. This transparency invites the partner to engage more deeply in the process, allowing them to feel included and valued. It also demonstrates a willingness to be vulnerable, which can strengthen the emotional bond. Rebuilding trust is also about patience. Trust takes time to develop, and it will take time to rebuild after being broken. Both partners should be prepared for setbacks and understand that healing is not linear. Celebrating small victories can be encouraging, fostering a sense of hope during challenging times. Acknowledging progress, no matter how minor, can help both partners stay focused on the journey ahead.

Engaging in shared activities can also contribute to rebuilding trust. Spending quality time together helps reinforce emotional bonds. This time can be used for creating new memories, establishing routines, or simply enjoying each other's company. Engaging in fun and meaningful activities can break down barriers and create a sense of connection. Whether it's taking a walk, cooking together, or participating in a hobby, shared experiences can help rebuild trust.

Seeking external support can be beneficial as well. Professional counseling or support groups can provide guidance and facilitate difficult conversations. These resources can offer insights into healthy communication patterns and coping strategies. Sharing experiences with others who have faced similar challenges can provide reassurance and help partners feel less isolated. Support systems can serve as valuable tools in the rebuilding process.

Reflecting on personal growth is another essential aspect of regaining trust. The individual in recovery should take time to assess their journey, acknowledging the lessons learned and the progress made. This self-reflection allows for a deeper understanding of themselves and their relationship. Sharing this reflection with their partner can open up meaningful discussions and further strengthen their bond.

As trust begins to rebuild, it is crucial to focus on the future. Creating shared goals and visions can help both partners feel invested in the relationship. Discussing aspirations, dreams, and plans can provide a sense of direction and purpose. Setting these intentions reinforces the commitment to working together, fostering a partnership grounded in mutual support and understanding.

Rebuilding trust after addiction is a journey filled with challenges and rewards. Each step taken towards healing creates a stronger foundation for the relationship. Through vulnerability, communication, and consistent actions, partners can restore trust and create a deeper connection. The process of regaining trust requires patience and effort from both partners, but the outcome is a healthier, more resilient relationship.

Navigating trust issues in romantic relationships and friendships can be particularly challenging after addiction. Trust, once compromised, can create barriers that hinder connection and intimacy. Individuals in recovery often find themselves grappling with lingering doubts, insecurities, and fear of betrayal. Understanding how to manage these trust issues is essential for fostering healthy relationships.

In romantic relationships, trust issues can manifest in various ways. A partner may feel insecure about their loved one's commitment, fearing that past behaviors will resurface. The recovering individual might grapple with feelings of unworthiness, questioning whether they deserve love and trust. These dynamics can lead to misunderstandings and conflicts, creating a cycle of doubt that can undermine the relationship. Open and honest communication becomes critical during this phase. Expressing concerns and feelings can help both partners gain clarity and understanding. Sharing vulnerabilities can bridge the gap created by past actions, allowing for deeper emotional intimacy.

Friendships also face unique challenges when navigating trust issues. The fear of being judged or rejected can inhibit openness. Friends may struggle to fully support one another due to their own experiences with addiction or recovery. Past betrayals can linger, leading to reluctance in fully engaging in the friendship. Establishing boundaries is crucial in these relationships. Friends should communicate their needs and expectations clearly, creating a safe space for both to express themselves without fear of judgment. By doing so, both individuals can work towards rebuilding trust and fostering a supportive friendship.

In both romantic and platonic relationships, it's vital to recognize the impact of triggers. Certain situations or conversations may evoke feelings of mistrust or anxiety, reminding individuals of past experiences. Awareness of these triggers allows partners to navigate challenges more effectively. Discussing potential triggers openly can help both parties understand one another's sensitivities, paving the way for more compassionate interactions. It's essential to be proactive in addressing these issues, rather than reactive. Establishing strategies for coping with triggers can foster a sense of security and understanding in the relationship.

Building empathy is fundamental when navigating trust issues. Understanding each other's perspectives allows partners to create a deeper emotional connection. Empathy encourages both individuals to consider how their actions and words may impact the other. It also promotes an atmosphere of support and understanding, which can be instrumental in overcoming past wounds. Practicing empathy requires intentionality and commitment. Both partners should strive to listen actively and respond with compassion. Engaging in open dialogues about feelings and fears can cultivate a stronger bond, allowing trust to flourish.

Consistency is another key element in navigating trust issues. The individual in recovery must demonstrate reliability and integrity in their actions. Following through on promises and commitments reinforces the message that they are committed to change. This consistency builds a sense of safety for both partners, allowing them to feel secure in their relationship. For friends, showing up during difficult times can strengthen the bond. Whether it's providing emotional support or simply being present, consistent efforts communicate trustworthiness and reliability.

Forgiveness plays a significant role in overcoming trust issues. Both partners must be willing to acknowledge the past and work towards healing. Forgiveness doesn't mean forgetting or excusing hurtful behaviors; rather, it's a conscious choice to let go of resentment and move forward. This process requires vulnerability and courage. For the recovering individual, it's essential to recognize that healing is a journey, and seeking forgiveness may involve more than just words. Demonstrating genuine remorse through actions reinforces the commitment to change and growth.

Setting realistic expectations is vital in navigating trust issues. Both partners should understand that rebuilding trust is not a linear process. There will be setbacks and challenges along the way. Embracing patience and compassion for oneself and one another is crucial. Celebrating small victories can reinforce progress and foster hope. Recognizing that healing takes time allows partners to approach trust-building with realistic expectations, reducing the likelihood of disappointment.

Engaging in shared experiences can help to navigate trust issues effectively. Creating positive memories together fosters connection and intimacy. Participating in activities that promote teamwork, such as volunteering or engaging in hobbies, can build trust and strengthen the relationship. These shared experiences serve as reminders of the bond created through mutual support and collaboration. Positive interactions can replace negative associations, allowing trust to grow organically.

Seeking professional help can be beneficial when navigating trust issues. Couples therapy or friendship counseling can provide a safe space for both partners to explore their feelings. A trained professional can offer valuable insights and tools for communication, helping to address underlying issues. In addition, support groups can provide opportunities to connect with others who have experienced similar challenges. Sharing stories and strategies can create a sense of community, reinforcing the idea that individuals are not alone in their struggles.

Self-reflection is also essential in navigating trust issues. Both partners should take time to assess their feelings, behaviors, and needs. Understanding personal triggers and insecurities can foster growth and empathy in the relationship. Self-reflection encourages individuals to consider how their past experiences shape their perceptions of trust. This awareness can lead to deeper conversations and a greater understanding of one another.

Finally, prioritizing self-care can contribute to navigating trust issues in relationships. Focusing on individual well-being creates a solid foundation for healthy connections. Engaging in self-care practices can help individuals manage stress and anxiety, allowing them to approach their relationships with a clearer mindset. Prioritizing mental, emotional, and physical health fosters resilience, enabling partners to navigate challenges more effectively.

Navigating trust issues in romantic relationships and friendships requires commitment, vulnerability, and patience. By engaging in open communication, practicing empathy, and demonstrating consistency, partners can work together to rebuild trust. The journey may be challenging, but the rewards of healthy, trusting relationships are well worth the effort.

Building trust after addiction is a journey that requires intentionality and dedication. Practical tools can help individuals and couples navigate this process, creating a solid foundation for trust and commitment. Commitment-building exercises provide opportunities for partners to engage meaningfully and reinforce their dedication to one another.

Creating a shared vision can be an effective exercise for building commitment. Partners should take time to discuss their goals for the relationship. This exercise encourages individuals to articulate their desires and aspirations. Writing these goals down can create a visual reminder of the commitment to work together toward a shared future. Revisiting this vision regularly fosters accountability and motivates both partners to stay on track. Additionally, it provides a platform for open dialogue about any challenges or adjustments needed along the way.

Another powerful exercise is the "Trust Ladder," which helps partners identify specific actions that contribute to trust-building. Each partner creates their own ladder, identifying behaviors that increase trust and those that diminish it. This visual representation can serve as a conversation starter, allowing partners to discuss their perceptions and feelings about trust. Working together to build a collective trust ladder can enhance understanding and create a shared commitment to support one another in their journey.

Engaging in regular check-ins can help communicate progress and reinforce commitment. Setting aside time each week to discuss feelings, concerns, and achievements fosters open dialogue. During these check-ins, partners should celebrate successes, no matter how small, while also addressing any lingering issues. This practice encourages both individuals to remain attuned to each other's emotional states and strengthens their connection. Consistent communication reinforces the message that both partners are invested in the relationship.

Incorporating rituals can also enhance commitment and trust. Simple routines, such as a weekly date night or morning coffee together, create opportunities for connection and intimacy. These rituals serve as a reminder of the bond shared and the commitment to nurturing the relationship. Partners should work together to establish rituals that resonate with both individuals, ensuring that they feel meaningful and enjoyable. Regularly engaging in these rituals can help partners feel secure in their relationship, reinforcing their commitment to one another.

Gratitude exercises can foster a positive atmosphere in the relationship. Each partner should take time to express gratitude for the other, acknowledging specific actions or qualities that they appreciate. This practice cultivates an environment of positivity, allowing partners to focus on the strengths in their relationship rather than the challenges. Gratitude exercises can be as simple as sharing three things they appreciate about each other during a designated time each week. Over time, these expressions of appreciation can build a deeper connection and reinforce trust.

Developing a conflict resolution strategy is essential for navigating challenges that may arise in the relationship. Partners should collaboratively establish guidelines for addressing conflicts in a constructive manner. This may include choosing a designated time to discuss issues, using "I" statements to express feelings, and actively listening to each other's perspectives. Practicing these strategies during low-stakes conversations can help both individuals feel more comfortable implementing them during times of heightened emotion. Establishing a clear conflict resolution process fosters trust, demonstrating that both partners are committed to finding solutions together.

Creating a "Commitment Contract" can also be a powerful tool for reinforcing trust and dedication. This informal agreement outlines specific actions and behaviors both partners agree to uphold in their relationship. The contract can include commitments related to communication, emotional support, and accountability. Writing this contract down and reviewing it regularly reinforces both partners' dedication to nurturing their relationship. The act of creating this agreement itself fosters a sense of partnership and responsibility, helping individuals feel more secure in their commitment.

Encouraging individual growth alongside relationship growth is crucial for building trust. Each partner should take time for self-reflection, identifying areas for personal development. Setting personal goals can enhance individual self-esteem and confidence, contributing positively to the relationship. Partners should support each other in pursuing these goals, celebrating achievements together. This practice reinforces the idea that both individuals are committed not only to the relationship but also to their own personal growth.

Utilizing journaling can provide a space for reflection and progress tracking. Partners can maintain individual journals to document their thoughts, feelings, and experiences related to trust and commitment. This practice allows for introspection, helping individuals gain clarity about their emotions and concerns. Sharing journal entries during check-ins can foster deeper understanding and connection. Journaling serves as a valuable tool for processing experiences, ultimately contributing to trust-building in the relationship.

Finally, seeking professional guidance can offer additional support in the journey of rebuilding trust. Couples therapy can provide a safe space for partners to explore their feelings and address underlying issues. A trained therapist can offer valuable insights and tools to navigate challenges, helping partners develop effective communication and conflict resolution skills. Engaging in therapy demonstrates a commitment to the relationship and a willingness to work through difficulties together.

Practical tools for commitment-building are essential for navigating the challenges of rebuilding trust in relationships after addiction. Engaging in shared exercises, rituals, and open communication creates a solid foundation for a healthy partnership. By investing time and effort into these practices, couples can foster a deep sense of trust and connection, paving the way for a fulfilling and resilient relationship.

Chapter 4: Boundaries: Protecting Your Recovery and Relationships

Establishing boundaries is essential in creating and maintaining healthy relationships, especially for those navigating the complex journey of recovery. Boundaries function as protective barriers, preserving personal well-being while fostering respect and understanding between partners. These limits are not merely rules; they are essential guidelines that allow individuals to express their needs, protect their recovery journey, and cultivate fulfilling relationships. Setting boundaries means defining acceptable behaviors, prioritizing emotional health, and ensuring that personal values are honored.

Understanding the importance of boundaries starts with recognizing their role in promoting personal autonomy. Boundaries empower individuals to take control of their lives, ensuring they are not overwhelmed by the expectations and demands of others. For someone in recovery, where the focus must be on sobriety, establishing clear boundaries becomes crucial. This clarity helps prevent distractions or temptations that could jeopardize the hard work put into maintaining sobriety. When individuals set boundaries, they communicate to themselves and others that their recovery is a priority, reinforcing their commitment to self-care and well-being.

Setting boundaries also facilitates healthier communication within relationships. When individuals have a clear understanding of their limits, it creates a foundation for open dialogue about needs and expectations. Effective communication nurtures trust and understanding between partners. When each person knows the other's boundaries, they can navigate potential conflicts with greater empathy and respect. This clarity reduces misunderstandings and the likelihood of resentment, fostering healthier interactions. In recovery, where emotions may be heightened and past traumas can resurface, clear communication becomes a lifeline that strengthens the relationship.

Identifying personal values and needs is a key aspect of boundary-setting. Each individual brings unique experiences, beliefs, and preferences to a relationship. Recognizing and articulating these values fosters mutual respect and understanding. Individuals should take the time to reflect on what is important to them and where they need to draw the line. This self-awareness is particularly critical in recovery, where external pressures can threaten personal well-being. Defining these values creates a foundation for establishing boundaries that align with one's authentic self.

Boundaries also protect individuals from toxic relationships that can impede recovery. Recognizing harmful dynamics is crucial for anyone in recovery. Toxic relationships can take various forms, including friendships, romantic partnerships, or familial connections. Establishing boundaries allows individuals to distance themselves from negative influences that may undermine their sobriety. This might involve limiting contact with individuals who engage in unhealthy behaviors or stepping back from situations that trigger temptation. By prioritizing healthy relationships, individuals reinforce their commitment to recovery.

Emotional safety is another crucial element fostered by setting boundaries. When individuals feel emotionally safe, they can express themselves without fear of judgment or retaliation. Creating an environment of emotional safety encourages partners to open up about their feelings, vulnerabilities, and struggles. This open dialogue fosters intimacy and strengthens the emotional bond between partners. Establishing boundaries around emotional safety means creating a space where both partners can share their thoughts and feelings honestly. This mutual understanding enhances the relationship, promoting healing and growth.

In addition to emotional safety, boundaries protect mental health. Individuals in recovery often face stress, anxiety, and past traumas that can impact their mental well-being. Boundaries create a buffer against overwhelming emotions or negative influences. They provide individuals the space to step back and engage in self-care, whether through solitude, therapy, or mindfulness practices. Prioritizing mental health is essential for maintaining sobriety, and boundaries offer the necessary space to nurture that aspect of well-being.

Establishing consequences for boundary violations is another essential aspect of boundary-setting. Clear consequences reinforce the seriousness of boundaries. Individuals must communicate what will happen if their boundaries are not respected. This may involve distancing themselves from a relationship, seeking professional help, or redefining expectations. Knowing that boundaries come with consequences encourages accountability and emphasizes the importance of respecting personal limits. This dynamic fosters a culture of respect within relationships.

For couples in recovery, setting boundaries can significantly impact relationship dynamics. Boundaries provide a framework for mutual support and understanding, allowing both partners to thrive individually and together. When partners respect each other's boundaries, it builds trust and encourages healthy interdependence. This mutual respect creates a sense of partnership, enabling both individuals to support each other's recovery journeys effectively. Boundaries promote a balance between intimacy and independence, fostering a relationship that is both supportive and empowering.

Practicing boundary-setting is a skill that requires time and patience to develop. Individuals should approach this process with self-compassion and understanding. Discomfort is natural when establishing boundaries, particularly if they have not been part of previous relationship dynamics. Taking small steps and gradually asserting boundaries can make the process more manageable. Individuals should remember that setting boundaries is an ongoing journey that demands consistent effort and communication.

In relationships where boundaries have been blurred or ignored, the process of re-establishing them can be challenging. Open and honest communication is critical during this phase. Partners should approach discussions about boundaries with empathy and a willingness to listen. This dialogue can serve as an opportunity for both individuals to express their feelings and needs, paving the way for healthier dynamics moving forward. Re-establishing boundaries may also require patience, as it can take time for both partners to adjust to the new framework.

The process of boundary-setting involves ongoing reflection and adaptation. Individuals should regularly assess their boundaries to ensure they remain aligned with their needs and values. Life circumstances, personal growth, and relationship dynamics can change over time, necessitating adjustments to boundaries. This ongoing evaluation allows individuals to stay connected to their authentic selves while navigating the complexities of relationships.

Establishing boundaries also fosters a sense of empowerment and confidence. When individuals take the initiative to define their limits, they send a powerful message to themselves and their partners: that they deserve respect and care. This empowerment extends beyond relationships, influencing how individuals view themselves and their capacity to advocate for their needs. As individuals learn to assert their boundaries, they develop a deeper understanding of their worth, which reinforces their commitment to recovery.

Ultimately, setting boundaries is about prioritizing self-respect and personal growth. Individuals in recovery must recognize their right to define limits and advocate for their needs. Boundaries empower individuals to take charge of their lives and protect their recovery journey. By establishing clear boundaries, individuals create a solid foundation for healthy relationships rooted in mutual respect, trust, and understanding.

Recognizing toxic dynamics in relationships is essential for anyone, especially for those in recovery. Toxic relationships can severely impact mental health, emotional stability, and the overall recovery journey. Understanding what constitutes toxicity allows individuals to identify harmful patterns, evaluate their relationships, and take necessary steps toward healing and growth.

Toxic dynamics often manifest in various forms, including manipulation, control, excessive criticism, and lack of support. Recognizing these behaviors is crucial for maintaining healthy boundaries and ensuring that relationships contribute positively to one's recovery. Manipulation, for instance, may involve someone attempting to exert influence over another's thoughts, feelings, or behaviors. This form of coercion can erode self-esteem, leading individuals to question their judgment and worth. In recovery, where self-affirmation and self-love are foundational, manipulation can be particularly damaging.

Control is another hallmark of toxic dynamics. In a controlling relationship, one partner may attempt to dictate the other's actions, thoughts, or decisions. This behavior stifles autonomy and fosters dependence, which can be detrimental to recovery. Individuals need the freedom to make choices that support their sobriety and overall well-being. Control undermines this freedom and can create a sense of fear or obligation. Recognizing these control tactics is essential for reclaiming agency in one's life.

Excessive criticism is often a subtle yet powerful form of toxicity. Criticism can take many forms, ranging from seemingly constructive feedback to harsh judgments that chip away at one's self-worth. In a recovery context, constant criticism can exacerbate feelings of shame and guilt, making it harder for individuals to embrace their journey. Learning to differentiate between constructive feedback and excessive criticism is crucial. Constructive feedback is meant to support growth and improvement, whereas excessive criticism serves to belittle and diminish self-esteem.

A lack of support in relationships can also signal toxic dynamics. Healthy relationships are built on mutual respect and encouragement. When one partner consistently undermines the other's goals or dismisses their struggles, it creates an environment where individuals feel isolated and unsupported. In recovery, support is paramount. Individuals must surround themselves with those who uplift them, validate their experiences, and encourage their growth. Recognizing when a partner fails to provide this support is essential for fostering a nurturing environment.

Toxic dynamics can be particularly insidious because they often develop gradually. Recognizing these behaviors requires self-reflection and awareness. Individuals should pay attention to how they feel in their relationships. Do they feel drained, anxious, or unsupported? These feelings can be red flags indicating that the relationship may not be healthy. Journaling thoughts and emotions related to specific interactions can help individuals gain clarity about the dynamics at play.

Identifying patterns in interactions is another critical step in recognizing toxicity. Do certain conversations consistently lead to feelings of frustration or hurt? Are there recurring themes of blame or guilt? Noticing these patterns can help individuals understand the dynamics at play and the potential for toxicity. Keeping a record of interactions can aid in recognizing these themes and inform future decisions about the relationship.

Establishing and maintaining personal boundaries becomes a crucial defense against toxic dynamics. Individuals must learn to communicate their needs and limits clearly. When boundaries are violated, it's essential to address the behavior directly. This confrontation can be uncomfortable but is necessary for establishing respect and understanding within the relationship. Individuals should not shy away from asserting their needs and expecting their partners to honor them. Having open and honest discussions about feelings is another effective way to address toxicity. Engaging in dialogue about specific behaviors that feel harmful can provide insight into the other person's perspective and foster a better understanding of each other's needs. It is important to approach these conversations with empathy, as the goal is to promote healing and growth, rather than blame.

Recognizing the impact of past experiences on current relationships is essential. Individuals who have experienced trauma, especially in the context of addiction, may find themselves drawn to toxic dynamics unknowingly. Patterns established in previous relationships can resurface in new ones. Understanding these influences can help individuals identify red flags earlier and make informed choices that support their recovery.

Engaging in self-care practices is vital for maintaining emotional health amid toxic dynamics. Prioritizing self-care creates space for reflection and rejuvenation. When individuals take time to care for themselves, they build resilience against negative influences. Self-care can take various forms, including engaging in hobbies, practicing mindfulness, or seeking support from trusted friends or therapists. By nurturing their well-being, individuals can approach relationships with a clearer perspective.

Therapeutic support can also play a significant role in recognizing and addressing toxic dynamics. Working with a therapist or counselor allows individuals to explore their relationship patterns and develop strategies for healthy communication. Professional guidance provides valuable tools for navigating challenging dynamics and reinforces the importance of self-advocacy. Therapy can be a safe space for individuals to process their feelings and experiences, ultimately fostering healthier relationships.

Empowerment is a key aspect of recognizing toxic dynamics. Individuals must feel empowered to make choices that protect their well-being. This empowerment involves understanding one's worth and the right to prioritize one's needs. Cultivating self-awareness and practicing assertiveness fosters confidence in addressing toxic behaviors. This confidence is vital in building a support network of healthy relationships that reinforce recovery.

Ultimately, recognizing toxic dynamics is about prioritizing emotional and mental well-being. Toxicity can take many forms, and individuals must remain vigilant in identifying harmful patterns. This awareness is an ongoing process that requires self-reflection, open communication, and the establishment of clear boundaries. By recognizing these dynamics, individuals can reclaim their power and foster healthier, more supportive relationships that enhance their recovery journey.

Learning to say no and set limits is an essential skill for maintaining healthy relationships, particularly for those in recovery. The impulse to please others often stems from a desire for acceptance and validation. However, when individuals prioritize others' needs over their own, they can compromise their emotional well-being and recovery journey. This dynamic can lead to resentment, burnout, and an inability to advocate for one's needs.

People-pleasing behavior can manifest in various ways. Some individuals may find themselves saying yes to every request, even when it conflicts with their priorities or values. This tendency often arises from a fear of rejection or abandonment. In recovery, these fears can be particularly pronounced, leading individuals to overextend themselves in an effort to gain approval or avoid conflict. A rehab counselor once joked with new patients, asking them if they were people pleasers. If they responded affirmatively, she would humorously suggest that they were "disgusting" and a "disgrace." While meant in jest, this comment highlighted the importance of recognizing people-pleasing tendencies as unhealthy and counterproductive.

Understanding that it is acceptable to say no is fundamental to overcoming people-pleasing behaviors. Saying no does not equate to being selfish or uncaring. Instead, it reflects self-awareness and a commitment to one's well-being. Individuals in recovery need to recognize their limits and prioritize self-care. By learning to assertively decline requests that may jeopardize their sobriety or mental health, individuals can reclaim their time and energy.

Setting limits is a crucial aspect of establishing healthy boundaries. Boundaries help define what is acceptable and what is not in a relationship. They allow individuals to communicate their needs clearly and ensure that their emotional and physical space is respected. Learning to set limits can be challenging, particularly for those who have internalized the belief that their worth is tied to their ability to please others. However, prioritizing self-care and well-being is vital for sustaining long-term recovery.

Practicing assertiveness is key to successfully setting limits. Assertiveness involves expressing one's needs and desires confidently and respectfully. Individuals should focus on using "I" statements when communicating their boundaries. For example, instead of saying, "You always ask me to do things for you," one might say, "I feel overwhelmed when I take on additional tasks." This approach emphasizes personal feelings and helps the other person understand the impact of their requests without eliciting defensiveness.

Self-reflection is an essential tool for understanding the motivations behind people-pleasing behaviors. Individuals should take time to consider their feelings when faced with requests from others. Do they feel obligated to say yes? Are they afraid of disappointing someone? Acknowledging these feelings can empower individuals to make choices that align with their values and well-being.

In addition to self-reflection, developing a strong support network can bolster individuals' confidence in setting limits. Surrounding oneself with people who respect boundaries and encourage self-advocacy can make a significant difference. When individuals have a strong support system, they feel more empowered to prioritize their needs without fear of judgment or rejection. This supportive environment fosters a sense of belonging that is healthy and nurturing.

Embracing the discomfort that may arise from setting limits is a crucial part of the process. Many individuals fear backlash or disappointment when they say no. However, confronting this discomfort head-on is essential for personal growth. In many cases, the other person may respect the boundary, leading to a healthier dynamic in the relationship. If they do react negatively, it is a reflection of their issues rather than a failure on the part of the individual setting the limit.

Engaging in role-playing scenarios can be an effective method for practicing assertiveness and limit-setting. Practicing responses to potential situations with a trusted friend or therapist can build confidence. Role-playing helps individuals prepare for difficult conversations and reduces anxiety when the time comes to assert their boundaries in real-life situations.

Setting limits also requires an understanding of one's priorities and values. Individuals should reflect on what is most important to them in their recovery journey. By identifying these priorities, they can assess whether certain requests align with their goals. For instance, if attending a social gathering conflicts with maintaining sobriety, it becomes easier to say no. Knowing one's values serves as a compass for navigating requests and obligations.

In some cases, individuals may encounter people who resist their attempts to set limits. This resistance can manifest as guilt-tripping, manipulation, or hostility. It is crucial to recognize that this behavior reflects their struggles and is not a reflection of the individual advocating for their needs. Maintaining steadfastness in the face of resistance reinforces the importance of self-advocacy and boundary-setting.

Learning to say no is a process that requires practice and patience. Individuals should approach this journey with compassion for themselves. Acknowledging that change takes time allows individuals to be gentle with themselves as they navigate new territory. Celebrating small victories—such as successfully asserting a boundary—can bolster confidence and motivation to continue setting limits.

Self-care must remain a priority in this journey. Taking time to engage in activities that promote well-being can enhance emotional resilience. Whether through exercise, hobbies, or relaxation techniques, individuals should create space for self-care practices that recharge and rejuvenate them. This intentional self-care can fortify the ability to set limits and say no without feeling guilty or overwhelmed.

Ultimately, learning to say no and set limits is a powerful act of self-love. By prioritizing one's needs and emotional well-being, individuals cultivate healthier relationships that support their recovery. This process empowers individuals to reclaim their lives, ensuring that their relationships are rooted in respect, understanding, and mutual support.

Setting boundaries is a critical aspect of maintaining healthy relationships, especially during recovery. The importance of having clear boundaries cannot be overstated. Individuals often find themselves caught between the desire to support loved ones and the necessity of protecting their own well-being. Practical tools for boundary-setting can provide essential guidance in navigating this complex terrain. One effective technique is to identify personal values, which serves as the foundation for understanding where boundaries need to be established. By recognizing what truly matters in one's life—whether it's mental health, physical well-being, or personal space—individuals can determine what behaviors and situations warrant boundaries. Writing down these values can serve as a reminder and reinforce the importance of maintaining them, making it easier to identify when a boundary is being tested. Creating boundary statements can also help in articulating needs clearly. A boundary statement should be simple, direct, and assertive. For instance, someone might say, "I need to focus on my recovery right now, so I can't attend social gatherings where alcohol will be present." This approach communicates the boundary in a respectful manner while also establishing a firm limit. Practicing these statements with a trusted friend can build confidence in expressing them during actual situations, making it easier to enforce them in the moment. Learning to say no is another crucial skill in boundary-setting. It can be particularly challenging for those who are accustomed to putting others' needs ahead of their own. Understanding that saying no is not selfish but rather an essential part of self-care is vital for personal growth. One way to practice saying no is by starting small. Saying no to minor requests allows individuals to become comfortable with the concept of setting limits. Gradually, this confidence can extend to more significant situations, where the stakes may be higher. It's important to remember that healthy relationships thrive on mutual respect. When one person asserts their boundaries, it encourages the other party to do the same, fostering an environment where both individuals can feel safe expressing their needs.

Another valuable exercise involves role-playing. Individuals can practice scenarios with a friend or therapist, taking turns in asserting and responding to boundaries. This technique not only helps in refining communication skills but also builds empathy, as participants understand the challenges and feelings associated with boundary-setting. Visualizing boundaries can also be a powerful tool. Imagining a protective barrier around oneself can help reinforce the importance of maintaining personal space and limits. Regularly practicing this visualization can serve as a mental cue during challenging situations, reminding individuals of their commitment to upholding their boundaries. Keeping a journal can also be beneficial in tracking progress and reflecting on boundary-setting experiences.

Writing about encounters where boundaries were tested can provide insights into patterns, triggers, and areas for improvement. This reflective practice allows individuals to adjust their strategies as needed and recognize the positive changes that occur when boundaries are upheld. Sharing experiences with a support group can further enhance the boundary-setting process. Engaging in discussions about challenges and successes in establishing limits helps normalize the struggle and reinforces the idea that others are facing similar issues. This communal support can serve as motivation to continue prioritizing personal well-being.

Creating a support network of friends, family, or peers who understand the importance of boundaries is essential. Surrounding oneself with individuals who respect personal limits reinforces the idea that setting boundaries is a healthy practice. It also creates an environment where individuals feel empowered to express their needs without fear of judgment or backlash. Encouraging open dialogue about boundaries within relationships fosters a deeper level of understanding and connection. These conversations can also clarify expectations and reinforce respect for personal limits, ultimately strengthening the relationship.

Maintaining boundaries requires ongoing commitment. As life circumstances change, so too may the boundaries one needs to establish. Regular check-ins with oneself and loved ones help ensure that boundaries remain relevant and respected. It's crucial to remain flexible while staying true to core values, allowing for adjustments as necessary. Practicing self-compassion throughout this process is equally important. Recognizing that mistakes may happen and that learning from them is part of the journey alleviates some of the pressure associated with boundary-setting.

Establishing boundaries can lead to a greater sense of autonomy and empowerment, enabling individuals to navigate relationships with confidence and clarity. By prioritizing their own needs and well-being, individuals in recovery can create healthier dynamics in their relationships.

Concluding this chapter, with its exploration of practical tools for boundary-setting, underscores the importance of establishing limits in the context of recovery. The techniques outlined, such as identifying personal values, creating boundary statements, practicing saying no, and engaging in role-playing exercises, equip individuals with the necessary skills to assert their needs effectively. The emphasis on maintaining open communication and fostering supportive relationships further enhances the ability to set and uphold boundaries.

Chapter 5: Romance in Recovery: Taking It Slow

Exploring romantic relationships with a fresh perspective is crucial for individuals in recovery. This stage often requires a reevaluation of what love, companionship, and intimacy mean. Many may have previously experienced relationships fraught with turmoil, codependency, or unhealthy dynamics, leading to a distorted view of romance. Recovery offers an opportunity to redefine these notions, emphasizing healthier patterns and nurturing connections.

In early recovery, the journey toward understanding what constitutes a healthy relationship begins with self-reflection. Individuals are encouraged to examine past relationships critically, identifying patterns and behaviors that may have contributed to their struggles with addiction. This reflection fosters awareness of unhealthy dynamics, such as co-dependency, manipulation, or emotional unavailability. Acknowledging these patterns is vital in preventing the repetition of past mistakes. The insights gained through this reflection can serve as a guide for establishing healthier connections moving forward.

Personal growth is a significant focus during recovery. Individuals learn to prioritize their own well-being and emotional health, which directly influences their ability to engage in meaningful relationships. The process of rebuilding self-esteem and self-worth empowers individuals to set higher standards for their partners and their relationships. They become more adept at recognizing red flags or behaviors that may indicate toxicity, leading to more conscious choices in their romantic endeavors.

In recovery, individuals often develop a deeper understanding of their emotional needs and desires. This newfound clarity encourages more honest communication with potential partners, facilitating healthier interactions. It becomes easier to articulate boundaries, expectations, and desires, leading to more fulfilling relationships. Honesty is not only crucial for self-expression but also fosters trust between partners, establishing a solid foundation for any romantic connection.

A fresh perspective on relationships also involves recognizing the importance of mutual support. In recovery, individuals often find strength in shared experiences, creating an environment where partners can encourage and uplift each other. Celebrating each other's victories, no matter how small, reinforces the bond and fosters a sense of teamwork. This support is essential as it helps both individuals navigate the challenges of recovery while deepening their emotional connection. Recognizing that romance does not equate to saving someone is another vital aspect of exploring relationships in recovery. The desire to be a savior can often stem from co-dependent tendencies. It's essential to understand that each individual is responsible for their own journey. Rather than stepping into a relationship with the intent to "fix" or "save" someone, partners should focus on mutual growth and support. This shift in perspective encourages individuals to view relationships as partnerships where both parties contribute equally to each other's well-being and recovery.

Furthermore, understanding that love can exist alongside personal struggles can redefine the approach to romantic relationships. Recovery does not eliminate the possibility of facing challenges; it instead provides individuals with the tools to cope and communicate effectively. Acknowledging that both partners may experience setbacks allows for greater empathy and patience within the relationship. This understanding fosters resilience, as couples can work through difficulties together rather than letting them become insurmountable barriers.

Emphasizing self-love as a prerequisite for healthy relationships is another critical element in this fresh perspective. Individuals in recovery must prioritize their emotional and mental well-being before seeking romantic partnerships. Developing a strong sense of self, understanding personal boundaries, and recognizing individual needs enable individuals to enter relationships from a place of strength rather than vulnerability. This self-awareness cultivates relationships that are built on respect, equality, and mutual support.

Exploring romantic relationships with a fresh perspective also encourages individuals to seek connections with others who share similar values and lifestyles. Engaging with individuals who prioritize their own recovery and well-being fosters a supportive environment. Shared experiences and common goals can deepen the bond between partners, creating a foundation built on understanding and compassion. Finding love among peers in recovery can be empowering, as both individuals work toward similar objectives and navigate challenges together.

Lastly, individuals are encouraged to embrace the notion that relationships can be a source of joy and fulfillment in recovery. While the journey may be fraught with challenges, it can also be filled with love, laughter, and meaningful connections. Understanding that relationships can enhance one's recovery journey rather than detract from it fosters a positive outlook. This perspective encourages individuals to approach romance with an open heart and mind, ready to embrace the beauty that love can bring into their lives.

The exploration of romantic relationships through a fresh lens enables individuals in recovery to redefine their experiences and expectations. It empowers them to build connections grounded in mutual respect, understanding, and support. By prioritizing self-love, emotional health, and open communication, individuals can cultivate relationships that contribute to their overall well-being and success in recovery.

Navigating romantic relationships during recovery presents a unique set of challenges that can significantly impact individuals' journeys toward healing. While love and companionship can offer support and motivation, they can also introduce complexities that may be overwhelming, especially in the early stages of sobriety. Understanding these challenges is essential for anyone seeking to balance their recovery with the pursuit of a meaningful romantic connection.

Addiction often disrupts emotional health, leaving individuals with a distorted sense of self and unaddressed issues. In early recovery, individuals may struggle with insecurity and low self-esteem, which can affect their ability to form healthy attachments. Past experiences of betrayal, abandonment, or trauma may resurface, complicating their ability to trust and connect with a partner. The emotional toll of addiction can create a fear of vulnerability, causing individuals to guard their hearts or, conversely, to become overly dependent on a partner for validation and support. In this fragile state, individuals may find themselves oscillating between craving closeness and pushing others away, leading to confusion and tension within the relationship.

Communication is another critical area impacted by addiction. Many individuals in recovery come from backgrounds where open dialogue was stifled or avoided. The fear of confrontation can lead to unhealthy patterns of communication, such as passive-aggressiveness or avoidance. In romantic relationships, this can manifest as an inability to express needs or feelings, resulting in misunderstandings and resentment. Healthy communication requires practice, patience, and a willingness to confront uncomfortable topics, which can be challenging for individuals still navigating their own emotions.

Another significant challenge arises from the need to establish boundaries. Recovery demands a focus on personal growth and well-being, making it essential to prioritize one's own needs. However, when romantic interests are involved, the desire for connection can sometimes blur those boundaries. Individuals may feel pressured to accommodate their partner's needs at the expense of their own recovery. This imbalance can lead to feelings of guilt or shame, creating a cycle that may ultimately jeopardize both the relationship and personal progress. The temptation to relapse can also be heightened in romantic situations. Relationships can trigger emotions and situations that remind individuals of past behaviors or environments. If a partner is not in recovery, the potential for exposure to substances or unhealthy coping mechanisms increases, posing a threat to sobriety. Maintaining a solid support system and prioritizing recovery activities is vital to resist these temptations, but balancing those commitments with the desire for closeness can create tension.

Financial stressors often accompany recovery, adding another layer of complexity to romantic relationships. Many individuals in recovery face economic hardships stemming from their past behaviors, including job loss, legal issues, or financial instability. Navigating these challenges while trying to build a relationship can strain partnerships and test commitment. Open discussions about finances and setting realistic expectations for shared responsibilities can help mitigate some of these stresses, yet doing so requires transparency and vulnerability.

Jealousy can become another obstacle in relationships formed during recovery. Individuals may project their insecurities onto their partners, leading to feelings of distrust and possessiveness. Such feelings can stem from personal fears of abandonment or inadequacy, intensifying emotions that are already heightened in recovery. Open and honest conversations about insecurities and expectations can help build trust and understanding. However, it requires both partners to be willing to engage in this dialogue, which can be difficult in the early stages of a relationship.

Forgiveness plays a critical role in romantic relationships, especially in the context of recovery. Individuals may carry resentment or bitterness from past relationships or experiences, which can hinder their ability to fully invest in a new partnership. The journey of recovery often involves addressing past hurts and learning to let go of grudges. This process can be challenging, as it requires introspection and a willingness to confront painful emotions. Healthy relationships thrive on mutual understanding, compassion, and forgiveness. Developing these qualities takes time, patience, and dedication from both partners.

Trust is another crucial element that can be challenged in romantic relationships during recovery. Individuals may find themselves struggling with trust issues stemming from past betrayals or disappointments. Building trust in a new relationship requires vulnerability and openness. Partners must be willing to share their fears, insecurities, and past experiences, creating a safe space for honest communication. Trust is not built overnight; it takes consistent effort and reliability to establish a solid foundation. The process of rebuilding trust often involves acknowledging past mistakes, making amends, and committing to being trustworthy in the present and future.

Co-dependency can also be a significant challenge in recovery relationships. Individuals may become overly reliant on their partners for emotional support, validation, or even sobriety. This reliance can create an unhealthy dynamic where one partner feels responsible for the other's well-being. Breaking free from co-dependent patterns requires self-awareness and a commitment to individual growth. Each partner must learn to prioritize their own recovery while supporting one another in their journeys. Establishing a healthy balance between independence and togetherness is essential for long-term success.

The temptation to romanticize recovery can also pose challenges. Individuals may idealize their partner's journey or see their relationship as a solution to their problems. This idealization can create unrealistic expectations and place undue pressure on both partners. Recovery is a lifelong journey filled with ups and downs, and it is essential to recognize that no relationship can serve as a panacea for personal struggles. Healthy relationships are built on mutual respect, understanding, and a shared commitment to growth.

Support systems play a critical role in navigating romantic relationships during recovery. Engaging with a community of fellow individuals in recovery can provide essential insights and encouragement. Sharing experiences, challenges, and triumphs with others can foster a sense of belonging and help individuals feel less isolated in their journeys. Couples in recovery should consider attending support groups together, as this can strengthen their bond and reinforce their commitment to sobriety.

Despite the challenges, the rewards of pursuing romantic relationships in recovery can be profound. Healthy relationships can provide emotional support, companionship, and encouragement, fostering personal growth and resilience. Individuals in recovery often find strength in the love and connection shared with their partners, which can motivate them to continue their journey toward sobriety. Building a partnership rooted in mutual respect, trust, and understanding can lead to a fulfilling relationship that enriches both individuals' lives.

Building relationships on new, healthy foundations is essential for individuals in recovery. This process involves a deliberate shift from past experiences to create connections rooted in respect, trust, and mutual support. As individuals embark on this journey, they must actively work to establish a solid framework for their relationships, focusing on the principles that promote emotional safety and personal growth.

Recognizing that the past does not define the present is a vital first step. Many individuals in recovery come from backgrounds where relationships were marked by chaos, manipulation, or co-dependency. This history can lead to skepticism about the possibility of healthy connections. By acknowledging these past experiences without allowing them to dictate current choices, individuals can start to break the cycle. Understanding that a fresh start is not only possible but necessary is empowering, allowing them to approach new relationships with hope and optimism.

Establishing boundaries is a foundational element in building healthy relationships. Boundaries create a framework for interactions, ensuring that both individuals feel respected and valued. This practice involves understanding personal limits and communicating them clearly to potential partners. Healthy boundaries prevent the erosion of self-worth and help maintain individual identities within the relationship. They allow individuals to express their needs while encouraging their partners to do the same. This mutual respect fosters an environment where both individuals can thrive without fear of losing themselves in the relationship.

Developing effective communication skills is equally crucial in establishing new relationships. Open and honest communication allows for the exploration of each partner's needs, desires, and expectations. This process encourages vulnerability, enabling individuals to express their feelings without fear of judgment. Healthy communication involves active listening, where both partners engage in conversations that foster understanding and empathy. This practice not only strengthens the emotional bond between individuals but also cultivates a culture of transparency, reducing the likelihood of misunderstandings or conflicts.

Trust is a cornerstone of any healthy relationship, and rebuilding it requires intentional effort. Trust is earned over time through consistent actions and genuine intentions. Individuals in recovery must be mindful of their behavior, demonstrating reliability and honesty in all interactions. Following through on promises, being accountable for one's actions, and showing respect for each other's feelings are essential components of building trust. As trust develops, it creates a secure environment where both partners feel safe to share their thoughts and emotions, deepening the connection.

Fostering emotional intimacy is another critical aspect of building relationships on new foundations. Emotional intimacy involves sharing vulnerabilities, dreams, and fears, creating a sense of closeness between partners. This depth of connection encourages partners to support each other through challenges and celebrate successes together. Engaging in activities that promote bonding, such as shared hobbies or meaningful conversations, enhances emotional intimacy. It allows partners to explore each other's lives more deeply, reinforcing the foundation of their relationship.

Acknowledging and celebrating each other's individual journeys in recovery is vital in building a strong partnership. Each person's recovery path is unique, with its own set of challenges and triumphs. Supporting one another in this journey creates a strong sense of camaraderie, where both individuals can celebrate each other's progress. Recognizing the importance of personal growth and development within the relationship fosters a culture of encouragement, allowing each partner to thrive independently while growing together.

Practicing patience is essential in building relationships on healthy foundations. Individuals in recovery often face setbacks, and the process of healing takes time. Understanding that progress may not always be linear encourages compassion and empathy. Partners should be prepared to navigate challenges together, offering support without placing blame. This patience reinforces the bond, demonstrating a commitment to the relationship despite the hurdles that may arise.

Being proactive in addressing conflicts is an important aspect of maintaining healthy relationships. Conflict is a natural part of any partnership, and how it is handled can significantly impact the relationship's trajectory. Establishing strategies for conflict resolution, such as using "I" statements and focusing on the issue rather than personal attacks, allows couples to address disagreements constructively. Engaging in respectful discussions fosters a sense of collaboration rather than competition, encouraging both partners to work together toward a solution.

Seeking support from outside resources can also enhance the process of building healthy relationships. Engaging in therapy, attending support groups, or reading self-help materials provides individuals with additional tools and perspectives to navigate their relationships. These resources can offer guidance on effective communication, boundary-setting, and conflict resolution, equipping individuals with the skills needed to create and sustain healthy connections.

Building relationships on new, healthy foundations involves a commitment to personal growth, effective communication, and mutual respect. By focusing on these principles, individuals in recovery can cultivate connections that not only support their healing journey but also enhance their overall well-being. This approach encourages a deep understanding of self and others, fostering relationships that are fulfilling, enriching, and rooted in love and trust.

Building healthy relationships in recovery requires practical tools that foster effective communication and the ability to recognize red flags indicative of unhealthy dynamics. Essential to this process is the art of expressing feelings and needs clearly. Utilizing "I" statements empowers individuals to communicate their emotions in a non-confrontational manner. For example, saying, "I feel overlooked when I share my thoughts," rather than, "You never listen to me," creates a more constructive dialogue. This approach minimizes defensiveness and opens the door for genuine communication, allowing both partners to engage without feeling attacked.

Active listening plays a crucial role in maintaining effective communication. Engaging fully with the speaker, demonstrating attentiveness through body language, and using verbal affirmations reinforces a connection between partners. Reflecting on what the other person has shared further validates their feelings and fosters mutual understanding. Phrases like, "What I hear you saying is..." not only show that you are actively listening but also create opportunities for clarification, enhancing the quality of the conversation. This engagement nurtures trust and intimacy, essential components in any supportive relationship.

Recognizing red flags is equally important in sustaining emotional safety within relationships. Awareness of behaviors that suggest unhealthy patterns helps individuals make informed decisions about their connections. Common red flags include persistent criticism, manipulation, excessive jealousy, and a lack of support for one's recovery journey. Identifying these warning signs early can prevent deeper issues from arising. For example, if a partner frequently undermines or dismisses your feelings, it may indicate a lack of respect and an unhealthy dynamic that warrants closer examination.

Establishing and maintaining healthy boundaries is vital for protecting one's emotional well-being. Clear boundaries define acceptable behavior in a relationship, allowing both partners to articulate their needs without fear of negative repercussions. Open discussions about boundaries can help ensure that both individuals feel secure and respected. For instance, if one partner feels uncomfortable with behaviors such as excessive texting or constant checking in, addressing these feelings can lead to a mutual understanding that fosters trust and respect.

Practicing self-reflection regularly is essential for personal growth and relationship improvement. Taking time to evaluate feelings, behaviors, and the overall dynamics of a relationship can yield significant insights. Journaling serves as an effective tool for articulating thoughts and emotions in a safe space. Reflecting on past interactions helps identify patterns that may need adjustment, facilitating healthier communication. Questions like "How did I feel during that conversation?" or "What could I have done differently?" can guide individuals toward self-awareness and improved communication skills. Seeking feedback from trusted friends or recovery allies is another valuable tool. Sharing experiences and inviting input from those who understand the recovery process can provide unique perspectives on relationship dynamics. Friends can help individuals recognize patterns they might overlook and offer guidance on navigating challenges. Those familiar with the recovery journey can provide both support and accountability, encouraging individuals to uphold healthy relationship standards.

Role-playing exercises can be instrumental in practicing communication skills within a safe environment. By simulating challenging conversations, individuals can build confidence and prepare for real-life interactions. This method allows for exploration of different approaches and helps individuals find effective ways to communicate their needs and boundaries. These exercises can be especially beneficial in honing active listening skills and developing empathy, critical elements for nurturing healthy relationships.

Incorporating mindfulness practices can further enhance communication skills. Mindfulness encourages individuals to remain present during conversations, reducing the likelihood of misunderstandings caused by distractions or emotional reactions. Techniques such as deep breathing can help calm anxiety before difficult discussions, promoting a more thoughtful and composed response. When partners approach conversations with a mindful attitude, they create a space conducive to open and honest dialogue.

Building healthy relationships in recovery is an ongoing process that requires commitment and practice. Utilizing these practical tools fosters an environment where both partners feel safe, respected, and understood. As individuals work to enhance their communication skills and recognize red flags, they lay the foundation for relationships that are supportive and enriching. By committing to these practices, individuals can navigate the complexities of relationships in recovery while fostering connections that promote healing and growth.

Navigating romantic relationships during recovery presents unique challenges and opportunities for growth, highlighting the importance of establishing healthy foundations and communication practices. By exploring romantic relationships from a fresh perspective and actively working to build connections based on respect and mutual support, individuals in recovery can cultivate relationships that enrich their lives and promote long-term sobriety. The practical tools discussed empower readers to recognize red flags and effectively communicate their needs, ensuring that their relationships contribute positively to their recovery journey. Embracing these concepts allows for deeper connections while prioritizing self-care and personal growth.

Chapter 6: Navigating Relationships with Family

Understanding family dynamics during recovery involves recognizing how addiction impacts not only the individual but also their loved ones. Families often experience a rollercoaster of emotions, from fear and anger to love and hope. These feelings can create a complex environment that influences the recovery process. In many cases, family members may have their own struggles with addiction, co-dependency, or mental health issues, further complicating the dynamics at play. The need for open communication and mutual support is essential as family members navigate their roles in the recovery journey.

Addiction can disrupt the traditional family structure. Family members may take on roles such as the enabler, the scapegoat, or the caretaker, often unconsciously. These roles can lead to unhealthy patterns of behavior that perpetuate dysfunction within the family unit. For instance, an enabler might feel the need to protect their loved one from the consequences of their addiction, inadvertently preventing them from facing the realities of their situation. Understanding these roles can help family members identify their behaviors and begin to shift towards healthier dynamics.

The impact of addiction can lead to a breakdown of trust within the family. Trust is foundational to any relationship, and when addiction is involved, it can be severely damaged. Family members may find it difficult to believe in the promises of recovery or to feel safe in their interactions. This breakdown can create a cycle of disappointment and resentment. Rebuilding trust requires patience, open communication, and consistent efforts to demonstrate commitment to change.

Family dynamics can also shift significantly after an individual enters recovery. The family may experience a sense of relief or joy, but this period can also be fraught with challenges. The newly recovering individual may need to establish new boundaries and patterns of behavior, while family members may struggle to adjust to these changes. Open dialogue about expectations and feelings is crucial during this transition. Families often need to learn how to support their loved one without falling back into old patterns that contributed to the addiction in the first place.

Effective communication is a cornerstone of healthy family dynamics in recovery. Each family member should feel safe expressing their thoughts and emotions without fear of judgment. Active listening is vital; it allows family members to understand one another's perspectives and fosters empathy. This practice can create a supportive environment where individuals feel heard and valued. Encouraging regular family meetings or check-ins can help establish a routine for open communication and foster connection among family members.

Understanding and addressing the emotional needs of each family member is critical in recovery. Family members may need support to process their feelings of hurt, betrayal, or anger stemming from the addiction. They may also struggle with their own guilt and shame about how they have responded to the situation. Providing resources for individual therapy or support groups can be beneficial. These spaces allow family members to explore their feelings in a safe environment and learn coping strategies that contribute to their well-being.

The concept of forgiveness often surfaces in discussions about family dynamics in recovery. While forgiveness is a powerful tool for healing, it can be a complex and challenging process. Family members may need time to work through their feelings and come to terms with the past. Understanding that forgiveness does not mean forgetting or excusing behavior is essential. It involves recognizing the pain and choosing to move forward in a way that promotes healing and growth.

As families work to understand their dynamics, establishing healthy boundaries becomes increasingly important. Boundaries create a sense of safety and respect within relationships. They allow individuals to express their needs while maintaining a sense of autonomy. Family members must learn to communicate their limits effectively and understand the importance of respecting one another's boundaries. This practice can lead to more balanced and supportive relationships.

Ultimately, understanding family dynamics in recovery is about fostering an environment of love, support, and healing. It requires patience, empathy, and a willingness to grow together as a family unit. As families navigate the complexities of recovery, they can emerge stronger and more connected, paving the way for a healthier future.

Family dynamics in recovery are complex and multifaceted, profoundly shaped by the impact of addiction. Understanding these dynamics requires examining how each family member interacts with one another and how their roles and behaviors shift in response to the challenges posed by addiction. Each member brings unique experiences and perspectives to the table, creating a tapestry of relationships that can either support or hinder the recovery process.

When addiction enters a family, it disrupts established patterns of behavior, often leading to significant changes in roles and responsibilities. For instance, a parent may shift from a nurturing figure to a controlling or enabling presence, while a sibling might take on the role of the family caretaker, sacrificing their own needs for the sake of the recovering individual. These changes can create a cycle of dysfunction that complicates the recovery journey. Recognizing and addressing these shifts is crucial for fostering a supportive environment.

Family systems theory provides valuable insights into how addiction affects relationships within the family unit. This theory posits that families operate as interconnected systems, where each member influences and is influenced by the others. In the context of addiction, this interconnectedness often leads to patterns of behavior that perpetuate the cycle of addiction and dysfunction. For example, a spouse may become overly dependent on the recovering partner for emotional support, while the recovering individual may struggle with feelings of guilt for the pain their addiction has caused. Understanding these dynamics allows families to identify unhelpful patterns and work toward healthier interactions.

The emotional toll of addiction on family members cannot be overstated. Each individual may experience a whirlwind of feelings, including anger, sadness, and anxiety. The burden of caring for a loved one struggling with addiction can lead to feelings of isolation and helplessness. Family members often grapple with questions about their own roles and responsibilities, feeling guilty for setting boundaries or frustrated by their loved one's choices. This emotional turmoil can create barriers to open communication, making it difficult for families to express their needs and concerns effectively.

Recognizing the importance of healthy communication is a key aspect of understanding family dynamics in recovery. Effective communication fosters trust and understanding among family members, enabling them to express their feelings and concerns without fear of judgment. By creating a safe space for open dialogue, families can work together to address the challenges posed by addiction and support one another in their recovery journeys.

Establishing boundaries is also vital in maintaining healthy family dynamics. Each member must understand their limits and responsibilities, ensuring that they do not overextend themselves in their efforts to support the recovering individual. Clear boundaries help prevent enabling behaviors and promote accountability, allowing everyone involved to focus on their personal growth and recovery.

Understanding family dynamics in recovery is a continuous process that requires ongoing reflection and communication. Families must navigate the complexities of their relationships while prioritizing the well-being of each member. By fostering a supportive environment grounded in understanding, empathy, and open communication, families can better navigate the challenges of recovery and emerge stronger together.

Healing hurt feelings and past wounds stemming from active addiction is a critical aspect of the recovery process for both individuals and their families. Addiction can inflict deep emotional scars on relationships, often leading to feelings of betrayal, resentment, and abandonment. The journey toward healing requires acknowledgment of these wounds and a commitment to rebuilding trust and understanding among family members.

The impact of addiction often manifests in various ways, creating a complex web of emotions. Family members may feel anger and frustration toward the individual struggling with addiction for the pain and chaos their behavior has caused. Simultaneously, the recovering individual may grapple with feelings of guilt and shame for their actions, leading to a profound sense of isolation. Understanding this emotional landscape is essential for facilitating healing, as it allows family members to recognize the shared pain and the need for compassion.

Open communication plays a pivotal role in healing hurt feelings. Family members must feel safe expressing their emotions without fear of retribution or judgment. Creating a space for honest dialogue enables individuals to voice their feelings, share their experiences, and articulate the ways in which addiction has affected them. These conversations can be difficult, as they often require confronting uncomfortable truths and painful memories. However, this process is essential for acknowledging past wounds and working toward healing.

The concept of forgiveness is often intertwined with healing. Forgiveness does not imply condoning the hurtful behaviors that occurred during active addiction but rather involves a conscious decision to release the emotional burden that resentment and anger create. For family members, forgiving the recovering individual can be a challenging journey. It requires patience, understanding, and a willingness to let go of past grievances. Likewise, the recovering individual must seek forgiveness from their loved ones, acknowledging the pain they have caused and taking responsibility for their actions.

Establishing boundaries is also vital in the healing process. Boundaries create a framework for healthy interactions, allowing family members to protect themselves from further emotional harm. For instance, a family member may need to communicate their limits regarding enabling behaviors or the conditions under which they are willing to engage with the recovering individual. Clear boundaries can help create a sense of safety and stability, fostering an environment conducive to healing.

Healing past wounds may also involve addressing specific incidents that have caused significant emotional pain. Family members might need to revisit difficult conversations or situations that remain unresolved. Engaging in these discussions can be challenging, but they are necessary for achieving closure. It is essential to approach these conversations with empathy and a desire for understanding rather than blame. The goal is to facilitate healing rather than rehash past grievances.

Practicing empathy is another crucial element in healing hurt feelings. Each family member's experience is unique, and fostering empathy allows individuals to understand one another's perspectives. Empathy involves listening actively, acknowledging each other's pain, and validating feelings without judgment. This process can help bridge the emotional divide created by addiction, fostering a sense of connection and understanding that is essential for healing.

Engaging in joint activities or therapy can also aid the healing process. Participating in family therapy or support groups can provide a structured environment for addressing unresolved issues and fostering open communication. These settings encourage shared experiences, helping family members navigate their emotions together and build a sense of solidarity in the recovery journey.

Ultimately, healing hurt feelings and past wounds requires time, patience, and commitment from all family members. It is a gradual process that may involve setbacks and challenges along the way. Recognizing that healing is not linear can help families navigate their emotions more effectively. Progress may ebb and flow, but the commitment to healing and rebuilding relationships remains paramount.

Creating new, positive experiences can also contribute to the healing process. Family members can work together to build a supportive environment where love and understanding flourish. Engaging in activities that foster connection and joy can help replace painful memories with positive ones, gradually reshaping the family's narrative. By prioritizing healing and understanding, families can create a foundation for lasting recovery, ultimately transforming the hurt caused by addiction into a journey of resilience and love.

Rebuilding relationships with family members who do not understand recovery can be one of the most challenging aspects of the healing process. When addiction affects a family, each member may react differently, and those who have not experienced addiction firsthand might struggle to grasp its complexities. Their lack of understanding can lead to miscommunication, frustration, and a feeling of isolation for the recovering individual. Acknowledging this disconnect is the first step toward rebuilding these vital relationships.

Open communication becomes crucial when addressing misunderstandings surrounding recovery. Engaging in honest and compassionate dialogue allows the recovering individual to express their journey, the challenges they face, and the positive changes they are striving to achieve. Family members may have preconceived notions about addiction, often influenced by stigma and misinformation. By sharing personal experiences and insights into the recovery process, the individual can help demystify addiction and offer a clearer understanding of their journey.

Patience plays a significant role in this process. Family members who do not understand recovery may need time to adjust to the changes and dynamics within the relationship. It is essential to recognize that healing takes time and that misunderstandings may persist. The recovering individual should remain patient while family members work to process the complexities of addiction and recovery. This patience creates a safe space for family members to ask questions, voice concerns, and express their feelings without fear of judgment.

Education is another powerful tool in bridging the gap of understanding. Providing resources, articles, or books about addiction and recovery can help family members gain insight into the experiences of their loved one. Understanding the physiological and psychological aspects of addiction can foster empathy and compassion, allowing family members to approach the relationship with a more informed perspective. Family members may also benefit from attending support groups, such as Al-Anon, where they can connect with others who share similar experiences and learn from their journeys.

Establishing boundaries is crucial when dealing with family members who do not understand recovery. The recovering individual may need to set limits on conversations or interactions that trigger negative feelings or reinforce harmful stereotypes. Communicating these boundaries with kindness and clarity can help protect the individual's emotional well-being. Boundaries provide a framework for healthier interactions, enabling the recovering individual to engage with family members on their terms.

Building trust is essential in rebuilding relationships. Family members may be hesitant to trust the recovering individual due to past behaviors and actions associated with addiction. Demonstrating consistency and accountability in daily life is vital to restoring this trust. Keeping promises, showing up for family events, and actively participating in recovery efforts can help rebuild credibility. Over time, these actions can demonstrate a commitment to change and a desire to foster healthier relationships.

Finding common ground can help strengthen the bond between the recovering individual and family members. Engaging in shared activities or interests can create opportunities for connection and positive experiences. These moments can serve as reminders of the love and support that exists within the family, despite the challenges posed by addiction. Rebuilding relationships requires an investment of time and effort, but the rewards of renewed connections can be profound.

Practicing self-compassion is essential during this process. The recovering individual may experience feelings of guilt or shame regarding their past actions and the impact on their family. Recognizing that recovery is a journey with ups and downs can help alleviate these feelings. It is essential to remember that the past does not define the future and that growth is possible through commitment and effort. Embracing self-compassion allows individuals to approach their relationships with a sense of forgiveness and understanding.

In some cases, it may be necessary to seek professional help to navigate complex family dynamics. Family therapy can provide a safe and structured environment for addressing misunderstandings and fostering open communication. A trained therapist can facilitate discussions, helping family members express their feelings and work toward mutual understanding. This professional guidance can be invaluable in rebuilding relationships that may feel fragile or strained.

Ultimately, rebuilding relationships with family members who do not understand recovery requires empathy, patience, and a willingness to engage in open dialogue. The journey may be fraught with challenges, but by prioritizing communication, education, and shared experiences, healing can occur. Each step taken toward understanding brings the family closer together, transforming past pain into a foundation for love and support. As relationships begin to heal, the recovering individual can foster a sense of belonging and connection, essential components of a successful recovery journey.

Rebuilding relationships within a family affected by addiction requires practical tools that can facilitate understanding and healing. Support-group involvement stands out as one of the most effective methods for family members seeking to comprehend the intricacies of recovery. By encouraging family members to attend support groups like Al-Anon or Nar-Anon, they gain insight into the struggles faced by those in recovery. These groups offer a safe space for family members to express their feelings, share their experiences, and learn from others who have walked similar paths. Hearing stories from individuals in recovery helps family members develop empathy and compassion, as they come to understand the challenges and triumphs that accompany sobriety. Such shared experiences can reduce feelings of isolation, making it clear that they are not alone in their journey.

Guided forgiveness exercises serve as another powerful tool in the healing process. Forgiveness does not imply that past hurtful behaviors are excused or forgotten; rather, it allows individuals to release the resentment and anger that may inhibit personal growth. Structured forgiveness exercises provide a framework for family members to explore their emotions related to their loved one's addiction. One effective approach involves writing a letter to the loved one, expressing feelings about the past and the impact of addiction on their lives. This exercise promotes catharsis, allowing family members to articulate their pain and frustration without the pressure of expecting an immediate response. Whether or not the letter is shared, the act of writing can be profoundly healing, encouraging emotional processing and paving the way for forgiveness.

Creating a family recovery plan is a practical step that can clarify roles and responsibilities for each member during the recovery journey. Collaboratively identifying goals fosters unity and reinforces the notion that recovery is a shared endeavor. A family recovery plan can include regular meetings to discuss progress, address concerns, and celebrate achievements, establishing a consistent forum for communication. This sense of structure can alleviate anxiety and create an environment of mutual support, enhancing the family's overall cohesion.

Incorporating mindfulness practices into family interactions can also strengthen relationships. Engaging in mindfulness exercises together helps cultivate awareness and presence, allowing family members to connect on a deeper level. Simple activities like deep breathing exercises, guided meditations, or even yoga sessions create a calming atmosphere that encourages emotional regulation. Practicing mindfulness together fosters understanding and empathy, allowing family members to approach discussions with a more open heart.

Participating in family activities that promote positive interactions is essential for rebuilding relationships. Dedicating time for shared experiences, such as family dinners, game nights, or outdoor outings, creates opportunities for connection and joy. These activities allow family members to create new memories together, reinforcing the belief that recovery is a journey taken as a unit. Focusing on the present moment during these interactions minimizes lingering feelings of frustration or resentment tied to past actions.

Seeking professional guidance through family therapy or counseling can also facilitate healthier dynamics. A therapist can help navigate complex family relationships, encourage open communication, and teach conflict resolution skills. Engaging in family therapy provides a structured setting where each member can express their feelings and perspectives, fostering mutual understanding. The therapist's role is crucial in guiding these discussions, ensuring that misunderstandings are addressed and encouraging constructive dialogue.

Additionally, establishing individual support systems for each family member enhances the collective healing process. Encouraging family members to seek therapy or join support groups allows them to address their emotions and challenges separately while contributing to the overall family dynamic. Individual therapy provides a space for family members to process their feelings, work through personal struggles, and develop coping strategies that can ultimately benefit their relationships. By fostering a culture of support and understanding, families can move forward together in their recovery journeys.

Rebuilding family relationships impacted by addiction is a challenging yet essential aspect of recovery. Through practical tools like support-group involvement, guided forgiveness exercises, mindfulness practices, and professional counseling, families can navigate the complexities of their experiences together. Emphasizing open communication and mutual support lays the groundwork for healthier dynamics, allowing individuals to express their feelings and heal past wounds. As family members engage in these practices, they not only foster understanding but also contribute to a shared commitment to recovery. By recognizing the importance of each person's role in the family unit, healing becomes a collaborative journey, reinforcing the notion that recovery is not an isolated endeavor but a path walked together.

Chapter 7: Forging Friendships That Support Sobriety

Building a solid support system is essential for maintaining sobriety. Positive friendships play a crucial role in recovery, offering encouragement, accountability, and a sense of belonging. Friendships formed during recovery can provide a unique understanding of the struggles and triumphs that come with this journey. These connections create a safe space where individuals can share their experiences without fear of judgment, fostering an environment conducive to healing.

Positive friendships serve as a buffer against the challenges of sobriety. They help individuals navigate the ups and downs, reminding them that they are not alone. Friends who understand the recovery process can offer valuable insights and share coping strategies that have worked for them. This exchange of support helps build resilience and strengthens the individual's commitment to sobriety.

Additionally, healthy friendships encourage individuals to engage in activities that promote well-being. Friends can inspire one another to participate in sober outings, such as hiking, attending support group meetings, or exploring new hobbies. These shared experiences reinforce the idea that life can be fulfilling and enjoyable without the use of substances. As friendships flourish, they can shift the focus away from past habits and onto building a future rooted in health and happiness.

The quality of friendships matters significantly in recovery. Surrounding oneself with individuals who have a positive influence can lead to healthier choices and behaviors. Toxic friendships, on the other hand, can pose a significant threat to sobriety. They may tempt individuals to return to old habits or undermine their self-esteem. It is essential to evaluate existing friendships and make conscious choices about who to allow into one's life during recovery.

Establishing boundaries with friends who engage in unhealthy behaviors can be a crucial step. It may require distance or, in some cases, the end of certain friendships. Prioritizing relationships that uplift and inspire fosters an environment where sobriety can thrive. Positive friendships can be the foundation for new, healthy relationships that reinforce the values of sobriety and personal growth.

In recovery, vulnerability is essential. Sharing personal experiences, fears, and aspirations with friends can deepen the bond and create a sense of community. When individuals open up about their struggles, it allows others to do the same, fostering mutual support and understanding. This vulnerability can lead to stronger connections and a sense of accountability, as friends encourage each other to stay committed to their recovery goals.

Moreover, friendships in recovery provide opportunities for personal development. Friends can challenge each other to step outside their comfort zones, explore new interests, and pursue personal growth. This growth often leads to increased self-confidence and a renewed sense of purpose. Positive friendships inspire individuals to envision a future that is not defined by their past but is full of possibilities.

Gratitude also plays a vital role in the dynamics of positive friendships. Expressing appreciation for friends who support recovery can strengthen the bond. Gratitude helps individuals recognize the value of these relationships, reinforcing the idea that they are not alone on their journey. Small gestures of gratitude, such as a simple thank-you or spending quality time together, can have a lasting impact on the friendship and the recovery process.

Engaging in sober social activities is another critical aspect of fostering positive friendships. Creating new memories without substances helps solidify the foundation of friendship built on shared values and experiences. Whether it's attending concerts, going for coffee, or participating in volunteer work, these activities reinforce the notion that life can be enjoyable without the influence of drugs or alcohol.

Participating in support groups also plays a significant role in forging friendships. Meeting others who share similar experiences creates a sense of community and belonging. These connections can lead to lasting friendships that extend beyond the support group, providing ongoing encouragement and understanding throughout the recovery journey.

Building a network of supportive friends takes time and effort. It requires individuals to be open to new relationships while being mindful of their boundaries. Recovery is a lifelong journey, and positive friendships are a crucial element in maintaining a healthy, fulfilling life. As individuals navigate the challenges of sobriety, the role of positive friendships becomes increasingly apparent, serving as a beacon of hope and a reminder that recovery is not a solitary endeavor.

Establishing new friendships during recovery presents unique opportunities and challenges. Individuals often find themselves at a crossroads, seeking connections that are supportive and conducive to their sobriety while navigating potential triggers. Recognizing the importance of forging new, healthy friendships is crucial in building a solid foundation for recovery.

Making new friends can provide a fresh perspective and invigorate one's social life, especially after the isolating effects of addiction. New relationships allow individuals to create connections based on shared values, interests, and experiences rather than old habits and destructive behaviors. Finding like-minded individuals can be both refreshing and reassuring, fostering a sense of community that reinforces recovery goals.

Exploring environments that promote sobriety can facilitate the formation of new friendships. Engaging in support groups, recovery-focused events, or sober social activities helps individuals meet others who understand their journey. These settings encourage open conversations and shared experiences, paving the way for meaningful connections built on mutual support. Friendships formed in recovery often come with an innate understanding of the struggles and triumphs of the process, allowing for deeper connections to blossom.

While building new friendships, it's essential to remain vigilant about avoiding triggers that could jeopardize sobriety. Triggers can manifest in various forms, such as specific locations, people, or situations that evoke cravings or negative emotions. Recognizing these triggers is vital for maintaining a safe environment during the process of making new friends. Developing awareness around potential triggers helps individuals make informed decisions about whom to engage with and where to spend their time.

Identifying personal triggers is the first step toward creating a supportive social circle. Triggers can be anything from the smell of alcohol to being around certain social settings where substance use is prevalent. By understanding what situations provoke cravings or negative feelings, individuals can set boundaries and choose friendships that foster a sober lifestyle. Communicating these boundaries to new friends can help establish a foundation of understanding and respect.

Building relationships based on mutual interests can also serve as a protective factor against triggers. When friendships are formed around shared hobbies, activities, or passions, individuals are more likely to engage in positive experiences that reinforce their commitment to sobriety. This approach creates a buffer against old patterns, allowing individuals to explore new avenues of connection while prioritizing their recovery.

Involving oneself in activities that promote wellness and personal growth is another effective way to make new friends while avoiding triggers. Joining fitness classes, art workshops, or community service groups not only fosters new connections but also encourages healthy habits that align with recovery goals. These environments provide opportunities to meet others who prioritize their well-being, thus reducing the likelihood of encountering triggering situations.

Having open conversations about recovery with new friends is vital. Sharing one's journey and the commitment to sobriety helps create transparency in the friendship. Friends who understand the importance of recovery can offer support, respect boundaries, and engage in activities that reinforce a sober lifestyle. This dialogue strengthens the friendship and fosters a deeper understanding of one another's experiences.

Patience plays a crucial role in making new friends. Recovery is a gradual process, and building meaningful connections takes time. Rushing into friendships without assessing compatibility can lead to negative outcomes. Allowing relationships to develop organically can lead to more authentic connections that stand the test of time. Friends should be individuals who genuinely care about one's well-being and respect the commitment to sobriety.

It's also important to recognize that not all friendships will be beneficial. Some relationships may inadvertently promote old habits or create a sense of pressure to engage in risky behavior. Evaluating the dynamics of new friendships is essential for determining their potential impact on recovery. Individuals must be willing to walk away from relationships that threaten their sobriety, even if it feels challenging.

Embracing the concept of quality over quantity is crucial in forming new friendships. A few strong, supportive friendships are more valuable than a large circle of acquaintances that may not have a positive influence. It's better to invest time and energy into relationships that uplift and encourage growth rather than spreading oneself too thin in less meaningful connections.

Navigating social situations can be daunting, especially when encountering friends from the past who may not understand the commitment to sobriety. It's important to have strategies in place for handling such situations. Practicing assertiveness and setting clear boundaries can help individuals feel empowered in social settings. It's okay to decline invitations or suggest alternative activities that align with a sober lifestyle.

Finding joy in new friendships is a rewarding aspect of recovery. Sharing experiences, laughter, and support with new friends can significantly enhance the recovery journey. Building a social circle filled with positivity and encouragement reinforces the idea that sobriety is not about isolation but rather about creating fulfilling connections.

Old friendships often carry the weight of past behaviors, serving as reminders of a time before sobriety and recovery. The challenge lies in recognizing that while these relationships may have once provided comfort, they can also pose significant risks to a person's journey toward lasting change. Familiarity can be a double-edged sword; on one hand, old friends may understand and accept you in a way that new friends do not, creating a sense of belonging. On the other hand, the shared history may include patterns of behavior that can trigger cravings or temptations to revert to old habits.

Navigating these relationships requires a deep understanding of personal boundaries and a willingness to reassess the dynamics involved. It's essential to identify which friends support your recovery and which may hinder your progress. For many in recovery, distancing oneself from toxic influences becomes crucial for maintaining sobriety. The emotional weight of past interactions can linger, reminding you of who you once were, but the decision to create distance is often necessary for personal growth.

Communication plays a vital role in this process. Being honest about your recovery journey with old friends may be necessary to foster understanding. Some friends may appreciate your openness and even support your journey by respecting your need for space or sobriety. Others, however, may respond with resistance or disbelief, making it clear that their lifestyle is incompatible with your new path. This can be painful, as it often leads to difficult conversations and potentially the loss of friendships that once held great significance.

It's important to recognize that friendships can evolve. If a friendship is rooted in shared past behaviors that no longer align with your values, it may be time to redefine the terms of that relationship. This could mean limiting interactions to environments that feel safe or opting to engage in activities that promote a healthier lifestyle. For example, meeting for coffee instead of at bars or social settings that encourage substance use can help create a more supportive dynamic. Over time, friendships can adapt to your new lifestyle, but both parties must be committed to fostering a positive relationship based on mutual respect.

In some cases, old friends may inadvertently act as triggers. Memories and shared experiences can evoke feelings that may lead to cravings or unhealthy thoughts. Recognizing these triggers is essential in making informed decisions about your social interactions. Developing a plan for how to handle these situations can be beneficial. This may involve practicing coping strategies, such as engaging in deep breathing exercises or having a supportive friend accompany you to gatherings where old friends may be present.

It's also crucial to cultivate a sense of self-awareness. Understanding your triggers and emotional responses can empower you to make choices that protect your sobriety. Developing new coping mechanisms and emotional regulation skills will equip you to navigate the complexities of old friendships with confidence. This might include engaging in journaling or speaking with a therapist, allowing for a deeper exploration of feelings surrounding these relationships.

As you continue on your journey of recovery, the focus must remain on creating a supportive environment that fosters growth. This may necessitate saying goodbye to some friendships while nurturing others that align with your sober lifestyle. It's okay to grieve the loss of these relationships; they may have played a significant role in your life and personal history. However, prioritizing your well-being and recovery is essential.

Building a network of supportive friendships is crucial in maintaining sobriety and fostering a sense of belonging. Meeting like-minded people who share similar values and goals can be a transformative experience. This process begins with actively seeking out environments where sobriety is celebrated, such as support groups, community events, or sober social gatherings. These spaces provide opportunities to connect with individuals who understand the journey of recovery and can offer encouragement and camaraderie. Attending events like recovery workshops or retreats can be a great way to meet people who prioritize their sobriety and personal growth, creating a shared foundation for meaningful connections.

Utilizing online platforms and social media can also facilitate the formation of supportive friendships. Many recovery-focused groups exist on social media, where individuals can share experiences, seek advice, and connect with others who are on similar journeys. Participating in discussions and engaging with others can help cultivate a sense of community. It's essential to be selective about the groups and conversations you engage in, ensuring they align with your values and support your recovery journey. Online friendships can be valuable, but making an effort to transition some of those connections into real-life interactions is important for building deeper relationships.

When forming new friendships, it's beneficial to approach interactions with an open heart and mind. Being vulnerable and sharing your experiences can foster deeper connections, allowing others to feel comfortable sharing their stories as well. Authenticity is key; showing up as your true self can attract individuals who resonate with your journey and values. This openness creates a foundation of trust that is essential for building strong, supportive friendships.

Navigating social situations can be challenging, especially when exploring new friendships. Communicating your boundaries and sobriety goals with potential friends is vital. A supportive friend will respect your needs and prioritize your well-being. Having clear conversations about what you are comfortable with regarding activities and environments will help establish mutual understanding. It's perfectly acceptable to suggest alternative plans, such as going for a hike instead of meeting for drinks or engaging in hobbies that promote health and well-being.

Additionally, it's important to cultivate existing relationships that support your recovery. Evaluating your current friendships and identifying those that uplift and inspire you can help solidify your support network. Nurturing these relationships requires ongoing effort, such as reaching out regularly, planning activities together, and being there for one another during tough times. A friend who understands your struggles can be a valuable source of support, providing encouragement and accountability as you navigate your recovery.

Practicing gratitude can also play a vital role in strengthening friendships. Taking time to appreciate the people in your life who support your sobriety fosters positive connections. Expressing gratitude can deepen relationships and create a culture of appreciation and mutual support. Whether it's a simple thank-you message or a heartfelt conversation about how much someone means to you, acknowledging their presence can enhance the bond you share.

Participating in sober activities can also help build a supportive community. Joining clubs or groups focused on shared interests, such as fitness, art, or volunteering, can facilitate new connections in a healthy environment. Engaging in these activities fosters interactions with like-minded individuals, reinforcing the idea that recovery can be a part of a fulfilling and vibrant life.

It's crucial to remain mindful of the ongoing nature of recovery and friendship-building. Relationships will evolve over time, and some may require reevaluation. If certain friendships no longer align with your recovery goals, it's important to acknowledge that and make necessary adjustments. Surrounding yourself with individuals who understand your journey and respect your commitment to sobriety creates a foundation for lasting connections.

In summary, building supportive friendships requires intentionality, vulnerability, and open communication. By seeking like-minded individuals, participating in sober activities, and fostering existing relationships, you can cultivate a strong support network that uplifts you throughout your recovery journey. The friendships you nurture will play a significant role in reinforcing your commitment to sobriety and enriching your life with connection and joy.

Chapter 8: Managing Romantic and Sexual Intimacy in Sobriety

Navigating vulnerability and emotional intimacy in recovery presents both challenges and opportunities for personal growth and connection. In the early stages of sobriety, individuals often grapple with the fear of opening up to others, especially in romantic contexts. The scars of past relationships, particularly those affected by addiction, can lead to apprehension when forming new connections. Emotional intimacy requires a level of trust that can feel daunting, yet it is a vital component for fostering healthy relationships. Recovery offers a unique chance to redefine vulnerability, transforming it from a source of fear into a pathway for deeper connections.

Vulnerability begins with self-awareness. Understanding your own emotions, triggers, and fears is essential before you can share them with someone else. This self-reflection fosters a sense of clarity, enabling you to articulate your feelings and needs more effectively. Journaling, therapy, or discussions with a trusted friend can aid in unpacking your emotions and preparing for open conversations with a partner. Recognizing and owning your vulnerability can be empowering. It creates a solid foundation for emotional intimacy, as both partners can share their authentic selves without fear of judgment.

Establishing emotional intimacy requires patience and practice. Engaging in deep, meaningful conversations is a vital step. Instead of surface-level interactions, delve into topics that matter to both of you. Share your hopes, dreams, and fears; explore what intimacy means to you and how it can be expressed in your relationship. Encourage your partner to do the same. This mutual exchange nurtures a bond built on understanding and respect. When both partners are willing to be vulnerable, emotional intimacy flourishes, allowing for a stronger connection that transcends physical attraction.

Navigating emotional intimacy also involves setting boundaries. Defining what intimacy looks like for you as individuals and as a couple is crucial. Discuss what feels comfortable and what may feel overwhelming. These conversations should be ongoing, as needs and boundaries may evolve over time. Clear communication regarding boundaries fosters a sense of safety, allowing both partners to explore vulnerability without fear of crossing unspoken lines. When both partners understand each other's emotional limits, it cultivates trust and encourages a deeper level of intimacy.

Forging emotional intimacy can also be enriched through shared experiences. Engaging in activities that allow for bonding, such as cooking together, hiking, or participating in recovery-based workshops, creates moments of connection. These shared experiences offer opportunities for emotional exchange and growth, reinforcing the bond you're building. As you navigate the challenges of recovery together, facing obstacles as a team fosters resilience and strengthens your relationship.

Another significant aspect of navigating vulnerability in recovery is recognizing and addressing fears of rejection and abandonment. Past experiences may leave scars, causing anxiety about how your partner may respond to your vulnerabilities. Remind yourself that everyone has their own insecurities and that opening up is a courageous act that can enhance your relationship. Acknowledging these fears within yourself and discussing them openly with your partner can alleviate tension and foster deeper understanding. Mutual support in facing fears can lead to a stronger connection.

Practicing empathy is essential when navigating vulnerability. Understanding your partner's feelings and experiences fosters a sense of safety and connection. When both partners practice empathy, it cultivates an environment where vulnerabilities can be shared freely.

This practice involves active listening, validating each other's feelings, and responding with kindness and compassion. When emotional intimacy is rooted in empathy, both partners feel valued and understood, reinforcing the foundation of their relationship.

As you build emotional intimacy, celebrate the small victories. Acknowledge the moments when you both share openly, express affection, or navigate challenges together. Celebrating these milestones strengthens your bond and reinforces the importance of emotional intimacy in your relationship. These celebrations create positive associations with vulnerability, making it easier to embrace in the future.

Navigating vulnerability and emotional intimacy in recovery can be challenging, yet it is a rewarding journey that fosters personal growth and connection. Embracing self-awareness, engaging in meaningful conversations, establishing boundaries, and practicing empathy can enhance the emotional bond between partners. By facing fears of rejection and celebrating shared experiences, individuals can build relationships that are not only grounded in love but also rooted in understanding and respect.

Ultimately, the journey of navigating vulnerability and emotional intimacy is one of courage and connection. It requires an ongoing commitment to open communication, self-reflection, and mutual support. As you cultivate these qualities within your relationship, you create a safe space where both partners can thrive emotionally and foster a profound sense of intimacy that strengthens your bond through the challenges of recovery.

Trust and open communication are foundational elements in intimate relationships, particularly for individuals navigating the complexities of recovery. Trust evolves from a series of consistent actions that demonstrate reliability and integrity. Rebuilding trust requires time, patience, and a willingness to be vulnerable. In recovery, individuals often carry the weight of past betrayals—both of themselves and of others. Acknowledging this history lays the groundwork for rebuilding connections. Transparency emerges as a vital component in this process. Sharing feelings, fears, and experiences opens pathways for mutual understanding. By engaging in honest conversations about triggers and challenges, partners create a safe environment where vulnerability can thrive. This willingness to share one's truth fosters an atmosphere of security, allowing both individuals to express their thoughts and emotions freely.

Effective communication intertwines with the rebuilding of trust. It involves more than simply exchanging words; it requires active listening and empathy. In recovery, partners must learn to articulate their needs and boundaries clearly. The art of active listening becomes crucial in this context, as it fosters genuine connection. This practice goes beyond hearing words; it encompasses fully absorbing the emotions behind them. Acknowledging feelings and responding thoughtfully cultivates a deeper bond. When partners actively listen, they send a powerful message: "Your voice matters."

The challenge of expressing emotions can loom large for those in recovery. Many individuals have learned to suppress their feelings, fearing vulnerability. To foster intimacy, partners should practice sharing their emotions openly. Designating times to discuss feelings—whether during quiet moments or structured conversations—normalizes emotional expression. This practice paves the way for deeper connections, where both individuals feel empowered to share their joys, fears, and insecurities.

Conflict resolution becomes an integral part of open communication. Disagreements are natural, and how couples navigate these moments can either strengthen or fracture their relationship. In recovery, conflicts may arise from external stressors or internal triggers. Adopting a collaborative mindset during disagreements promotes understanding rather than competition. Seeking common ground allows both partners to feel validated. Utilizing "I" statements can help frame discussions around feelings rather than accusations, promoting a more constructive dialogue.

As trust builds and communication deepens, emotional intimacy flourishes. Vulnerability becomes a strength rather than a liability. Sharing past experiences, discussing fears about the future, and expressing insecurities allow partners to support one another in their healing journeys. The understanding that both individuals are working toward personal growth fosters unity and connection.

Trust also extends into the realm of physical intimacy. Establishing a safe space for physical affection is essential, especially for those grappling with feelings of shame tied to past behaviors. Open discussions about boundaries and desires are crucial for creating an environment where both partners feel comfortable expressing their physical affection. This dialogue empowers individuals to communicate their needs and comfort levels, ensuring that both partners are aligned.

Nurturing trust requires ongoing effort from both partners. Small acts of kindness, keeping promises, and expressing appreciation reinforce the bond. Regular check-ins about each partner's feelings and needs help maintain open communication. These practices foster a culture of mutual support, reinforcing the commitment to each other's well-being.

The journey of developing trust and open communication in intimate relationships is one of growth and connection. It requires a commitment to honesty, compassion, and a willingness to confront challenges together. As couples embrace these principles, they not only strengthen their relationship but also enhance their individual recovery journeys. Trust and communication serve as the bedrock upon which healthy, fulfilling partnerships can flourish, allowing love to blossom in the midst of adversity.

Reintroducing physical intimacy in recovery requires a thoughtful, compassionate approach that prioritizes both partners' comfort and emotional safety. The journey toward intimacy often begins with a deep understanding of individual boundaries. Before engaging in physical affection, it's essential for both partners to have open discussions about their comfort levels, desires, and any concerns they may harbor. This initial conversation establishes a foundation of trust and transparency, enabling each person to voice their feelings honestly without fear of judgment. Understanding each other's past experiences with intimacy, especially in the context of addiction and recovery, creates an opportunity to foster mutual empathy.

Recognizing that vulnerability is inherent in physical intimacy is vital. Those in recovery may carry baggage from past relationships that can complicate their feelings about touch and affection. It's common for individuals to feel shame or anxiety surrounding physical closeness due to prior experiences. Partners must approach these feelings with sensitivity and patience. Creating a safe space where both individuals feel heard and validated allows for healing and the gradual rebuilding of intimacy. Discussing what physical intimacy means to each partner can help navigate differing expectations and fears.

Start by incorporating non-sexual forms of physical touch. Simple gestures like holding hands, hugging, or cuddling can help rebuild a sense of physical connection without the pressure of sexual expectations. These acts of affection can serve as stepping stones toward deeper intimacy, allowing both partners to gradually acclimate to physical closeness. The emphasis should be on enjoyment and connection rather than performance, freeing both individuals from the constraints of previous experiences.

Establishing clear boundaries is essential as physical intimacy is reintroduced. Each partner should define their comfort zones and express any limits they wish to maintain. This dialogue can be ongoing, with regular check-ins about how each person feels. Acknowledging that boundaries may evolve over time is crucial, as recovery is a dynamic process. By maintaining an open line of communication, partners can navigate changes and adapt their approach to intimacy as their relationship grows.

Creating a romantic atmosphere can enhance the experience of physical intimacy. This doesn't necessarily require elaborate planning; it can be as simple as lighting candles, playing soft music, or enjoying a quiet moment together. These elements help set a tone of warmth and connection, allowing both partners to relax and feel more comfortable with each other. When the environment feels nurturing, individuals are more likely to open up to the idea of physical closeness.

Mindfulness can also play a significant role in reintroducing physical intimacy. Practicing mindfulness encourages both partners to focus on the present moment, enhancing their awareness of sensations and emotions. Engaging in mindfulness exercises together, such as deep breathing or meditation, can help ease anxiety and foster a sense of connection. As they become more attuned to each other's feelings, partners can better navigate the complexities of intimacy, allowing them to respond to each other's needs in real time.

Addressing fears or insecurities regarding physical intimacy is essential. It's common for individuals in recovery to harbor concerns about their worthiness of love and affection. Encouraging open dialogue about these fears fosters a supportive environment. Reassuring one another of their commitment and love can help alleviate anxiety and build confidence in the relationship. This support is crucial in allowing both partners to explore intimacy without the weight of past traumas overshadowing their experience.

It's also vital to approach intimacy at a pace that feels comfortable for both partners. Rushing into physical closeness can trigger feelings of anxiety or insecurity, potentially derailing the progress made in recovery. By taking things slow, partners can build anticipation and excitement, enhancing the emotional connection that underlies physical intimacy. Each small step taken together reinforces the bond, creating a solid foundation upon which deeper intimacy can flourish.

Educating oneself about healthy sexual practices can be empowering for both partners. Understanding consent, safe sex practices, and the importance of mutual satisfaction can alleviate anxieties surrounding sexual intimacy. This knowledge fosters a sense of control and confidence, allowing partners to engage more freely in intimate experiences. Couples should take the time to explore each other's preferences, desires, and boundaries, ensuring that both feel respected and valued in the relationship.

As partners navigate the complexities of physical intimacy, celebrating each other's progress becomes essential. Acknowledging the small victories—whether it's a simple touch, a shared moment of laughter, or a successful intimate encounter—reinforces the emotional connection between partners. Celebrating these milestones fosters positivity and strengthens the foundation of the relationship, emphasizing that intimacy is a journey rather than a destination.

Finally, remaining attuned to one's own emotional and physical state throughout this process is crucial. Individuals in recovery may find that their feelings about intimacy fluctuate, and that's perfectly normal. Encouraging self-reflection can help partners recognize their needs and feelings, allowing them to communicate more effectively with each other. Prioritizing self-care—whether through therapy, journaling, or engaging in hobbies—can enhance emotional well-being, contributing to a healthier dynamic within the relationship.

Reintroducing physical intimacy in sobriety is a journey that requires patience, communication, and empathy. By prioritizing open dialogue, establishing boundaries, and creating a supportive environment, partners can gradually rebuild intimacy while respecting each other's feelings and experiences. This journey, rooted in trust and understanding, ultimately fosters a deeper emotional connection, allowing love to flourish in a safe and nurturing space. As both partners embrace this process, they discover the beauty of intimacy rooted in respect, vulnerability, and a shared commitment to one another's recovery.

Creating safe spaces within a romantic relationship is a foundational element that fosters emotional safety and intimacy, especially in the context of recovery. It begins with the intention of establishing an environment where both partners feel valued, respected, and free to express their emotions without fear of judgment or retribution. To cultivate this atmosphere, clear communication is paramount. Engaging in ongoing dialogues about feelings, needs, and boundaries allows both partners to understand each other better and reinforces the idea that their relationship is a safe haven.

Setting aside regular times to check in with each other can help ensure that both partners feel heard and understood. These check-ins can take various forms—whether during a quiet moment at home, a walk in nature, or over a cup of coffee. The key is to create a routine that encourages open communication, allowing both individuals to share their thoughts and feelings. During these conversations, it's essential to approach the dialogue with curiosity rather than defensiveness. Partners should practice active listening, which involves not just hearing the words but also being attuned to the emotions and intentions behind them. This level of engagement fosters a deeper understanding and strengthens the bond between partners.

To establish boundaries that protect each partner's emotional well-being, it's crucial to discuss and agree on what those boundaries entail. Boundaries are not about building walls but about creating guidelines that ensure both individuals feel comfortable and respected. These boundaries might encompass topics such as emotional triggers, communication styles, and personal space. Partners should take the time to articulate their needs clearly, discussing what behaviors are acceptable and what may be hurtful or triggering. This process of boundary-setting can be an ongoing conversation, with both partners encouraged to voice any changes as their relationship evolves.

When establishing boundaries, it's important to recognize that they may not be one-size-fits-all. Each partner comes with their unique set of experiences and vulnerabilities, and their boundaries should reflect that individuality. For instance, one partner may need more space to process emotions, while the other may thrive on frequent affirmations and closeness. By being open to discussing these differences, partners can negotiate boundaries that honor both individuals' needs.

Creating safe spaces can also involve cultivating an atmosphere of non-judgment. Both partners must commit to being compassionate listeners and avoiding criticism when discussing sensitive topics. Encouraging a culture of acceptance helps build trust, allowing both individuals to explore their vulnerabilities without the fear of being dismissed or belittled. It's essential to recognize that everyone has different ways of coping and processing emotions, and understanding these differences is key to fostering a safe environment.

Another practical tool is to establish rituals that promote connection and safety within the relationship. Rituals can be simple yet powerful practices that reinforce the bond between partners. These might include weekly date nights, morning check-ins, or shared hobbies that allow both partners to unwind and reconnect. Engaging in rituals that promote positivity helps create a shared sense of purpose and belonging. When partners invest in these shared experiences, they reinforce the idea that their relationship is a safe haven where they can be themselves without pretense.

Engaging in vulnerability exercises can also help partners cultivate emotional safety. Vulnerability exercises encourage both individuals to share their fears, dreams, and insecurities in a structured manner. This process might involve each partner writing down their thoughts and sharing them in a safe setting. By practicing vulnerability together, partners develop empathy and a deeper understanding of each other's struggles, fostering a stronger emotional connection. This mutual sharing reinforces the idea that both partners are committed to navigating the complexities of intimacy and recovery together.

Another essential aspect of creating safe spaces is recognizing the role of physical safety in emotional intimacy. Both partners must be comfortable with their physical interactions and ensure that touch is consensual and respectful. Establishing boundaries around physical affection is crucial, especially in the early stages of reintroducing intimacy. Partners should openly communicate their comfort levels regarding physical touch, whether it's cuddling, holding hands, or more intimate expressions of affection. This ongoing dialogue helps both individuals feel empowered to express their needs and preferences without fear of overstepping boundaries.

Ensuring that boundaries are respected is a continual process that requires vigilance and commitment from both partners. Regularly revisiting boundary discussions can help both individuals assess how they feel about their current boundaries and whether any adjustments are needed. It's important for partners to approach these conversations with a spirit of cooperation rather than confrontation, emphasizing the shared goal of nurturing a healthy, supportive relationship.

If a partner feels that their boundaries have been crossed, it's crucial to address these feelings promptly. Ignoring feelings of discomfort can lead to resentment and distance within the relationship. Instead, both partners should engage in a candid conversation about what happened, allowing the affected individual to express their feelings without fear of retaliation. By addressing boundary violations openly, both partners can work toward restoring trust and reinforcing the importance of mutual respect within the relationship.

In addition to open dialogue, couples can also engage in specific exercises that help reinforce their commitment to creating a safe space. These exercises might include expressing gratitude for one another, acknowledging each other's strengths, and reaffirming their love and commitment. Such practices foster positivity within the relationship and encourage both partners to remain focused on the elements that strengthen their bond.

Another practical tool for ensuring emotional safety is setting aside technology-free time. In an age where digital distractions can often pull attention away from meaningful interactions, designating specific times for tech-free connection can be beneficial. This practice encourages partners to engage with each other fully, enhancing the quality of their communication and reinforcing their emotional connection.

To support the creation of safe spaces, partners should also consider seeking outside resources, such as therapy or support groups, if needed. Professional guidance can provide valuable insights and tools for navigating the complexities of intimacy and recovery. These resources can help couples understand the nuances of their relationship dynamics and equip them with strategies for fostering emotional safety.

Ultimately, the goal of creating safe spaces and ensuring boundaries in a romantic relationship is to cultivate a nurturing environment where both partners can thrive. This journey requires ongoing commitment, open communication, and a willingness to embrace vulnerability. By actively working to establish emotional safety and respect for one another's boundaries, partners can lay the groundwork for a healthy, fulfilling relationship that supports both individuals' recovery journeys. Acknowledging that this process is not always linear and that challenges may arise along the way is important. However, with a shared commitment to growth and understanding, partners can forge a path toward deeper emotional intimacy and connection in sobriety.

Chapter 9: THE BIG ONE Co-Dependency vs. Healthy Dependency

Understanding the distinction between supportive and co-dependent relationships is foundational in the journey of recovery and personal growth. Supportive relationships are characterized by mutual respect, where both partners encourage each other to pursue individual interests, aspirations, and emotional well-being. In these healthy dynamics, partners are secure in their identities and celebrate one another's successes without feeling threatened or diminished. The focus remains on fostering each other's strengths while also addressing weaknesses with empathy and understanding. Healthy partners communicate openly, establishing a safe space for vulnerability and growth.

In contrast, co-dependent relationships often emerge from insecurities and unhealthy attachments. These relationships are marked by an imbalance, where one partner's well-being becomes overly dependent on the other. This dynamic often manifests as one partner sacrificing their needs, desires, and interests for the sake of the other. Such dependence can create a cycle of enabling behaviors, where one individual's struggles with addiction or emotional distress lead to the other partner feeling responsible for their happiness and recovery. This sense of obligation can stifle personal growth, leading to resentment, frustration, and ultimately, the deterioration of both individuals' mental health.

Recognizing the signs of co-dependency is crucial for anyone navigating relationships during recovery. These signs may include a lack of personal boundaries, feelings of guilt or anxiety when prioritizing one's needs, and a tendency to rescue or fix one's partner. Additionally, communication in co-dependent relationships may be marked by avoidance of difficult conversations, a fear of rejection, or an overwhelming need for approval. Individuals often find themselves trapped in a cycle of caretaking, which may ultimately hinder the recovery process for both partners.

Supportive relationships, on the other hand, create an environment where individuals can thrive. In these connections, partners actively listen and validate each other's experiences, fostering a sense of belonging and acceptance. They share responsibilities and engage in constructive conflict resolution, ensuring that both voices are heard and valued. Emotional intimacy is built through honest communication, where partners can express their vulnerabilities without fear of judgment. This safe space allows each person to grow both independently and as a couple, contributing to a healthier relational dynamic.

The journey from co-dependency to a supportive relationship can be challenging but incredibly rewarding. It often involves self-reflection, personal growth, and open dialogue about each partner's needs and desires. Couples may need to engage in difficult conversations to dismantle patterns of behavior that have become ingrained over time. Seeking therapy or counseling can provide essential tools and strategies to facilitate this transition, equipping partners with the skills to communicate effectively and set healthy boundaries.

Ultimately, the goal is to foster a relationship that allows both partners to flourish individually while providing a strong support system for one another. By embracing the principles of respect, empathy, and open communication, couples can cultivate a relationship dynamic that enhances their recovery journey and strengthens their emotional bonds.

Understanding the nuances between supportive and co-dependent relationships proves crucial in recovery, especially for those who have struggled with addiction. At its core, a supportive relationship fosters mutual respect, trust, and a sense of balance, where both partners contribute to each other's well-being while maintaining their individual identities. Supportive relationships are characterized by encouragement, communication, and emotional availability. Both partners feel safe expressing their thoughts and feelings, knowing they will be met with understanding and empathy. This environment allows individuals to grow both as partners and as individuals, creating a space where both can thrive without sacrificing their needs or identities. Supportive relationships cultivate interdependence, where both partners rely on each other in healthy ways that promote mutual growth and healing.

Co-dependent relationships often blur the lines between love and control, leading to unhealthy dynamics that hinder personal growth and recovery. Co-dependency typically arises from fear, control, and an unhealthy reliance on another person for self-worth and identity. In these dynamics, one partner may feel responsible for the other's feelings, actions, and recovery journey, leading to a cycle of enabling behaviors. This manifests as one partner consistently prioritizing the other's needs over their own, sacrificing their well-being to maintain the relationship. Over time, this dynamic results in resentment, burnout, and a loss of self for both individuals.

In recovery, recognizing the signs of co-dependency early on prevents these unhealthy patterns from taking root. Individuals may find themselves in co-dependent relationships if they constantly feel responsible for their partner's emotions or recovery. Feelings of guilt may surface when they pursue their interests or self-care, fearing it will upset their partner. The partner relying heavily on another for emotional support often struggles with feelings of inadequacy or anxiety when alone. Recognizing these signs helps individuals discern whether their relationships are genuinely supportive or veering into co-dependent territory.

Co-dependency exacerbates challenges faced in recovery. When one partner struggles with addiction, the other may inadvertently become an enabler by assuming responsibility for their partner's recovery. This toxic cycle leads the addicted partner to feel less motivated to change while the other partner becomes emotionally drained and resentful. In a healthy relationship, both partners support each other in their recovery journeys, understanding that each individual's growth holds equal importance.

Building supportive relationships begins with open communication. Partners should express their needs and desires, fostering an environment where both individuals feel valued and heard. Regular check-ins about feelings and concerns can strengthen the emotional connection and prevent misunderstandings from escalating into resentment. Practicing active listening enhances understanding and reinforces emotional safety within the relationship.

Setting boundaries becomes essential in distinguishing between supportive and co-dependent behaviors. Healthy boundaries help individuals define their own needs while respecting those of their partners. Establishing these limits prevents one partner from feeling overwhelmed or burdened by the other's emotional state. Healthy relationships thrive on mutual respect, where each partner recognizes the other's autonomy and individuality.

Self-awareness plays a crucial role in nurturing supportive relationships. Both partners should reflect on their own behaviors and motivations, identifying any patterns that may lean toward co-dependency. Engaging in self-reflection helps individuals understand their triggers and emotional responses, allowing them to address issues before they affect the relationship. Personal growth outside the relationship is equally important. Pursuing individual interests and hobbies fosters a sense of identity separate from the partnership, strengthening both partners' overall well-being.

Seeking external support can also be beneficial in navigating the complexities of supportive versus co-dependent relationships. Engaging with therapy or support groups provides individuals with tools to identify unhealthy patterns and develop healthier coping mechanisms. Professional guidance allows partners to explore their dynamics in a safe space, encouraging open dialogue about feelings, needs, and concerns. As individuals work on their personal growth, they can bring that progress back into the relationship, contributing to a healthier partnership.

Trust serves as the foundation for any supportive relationship. Building and maintaining trust requires transparency and honesty. Partners must feel secure in sharing their thoughts and emotions without fear of judgment or backlash. Establishing trust takes time and consistency, as both partners demonstrate reliability in their words and actions. Trust is reinforced through open communication, where both partners feel free to express their vulnerabilities.

Recognizing the importance of mutual support in recovery strengthens relationships. Partners should celebrate each other's achievements, no matter how small, as this fosters a sense of teamwork and unity. Encouragement serves as a powerful motivator for both partners, creating an environment where individuals feel empowered to pursue their recovery journeys together. Supporting each other's goals cultivates a shared sense of purpose, reinforcing the bond between partners.

Understanding the balance between dependence and independence becomes vital in nurturing supportive relationships. While it's natural to lean on each other for emotional support, partners must also maintain their independence. Encouraging one another to pursue individual passions and friendships enhances the partnership. Embracing both independence and togetherness creates a harmonious balance that benefits both partners and strengthens their relationship.

Ultimately, the journey from co-dependency to healthy dependency requires commitment and effort from both partners. Recognizing the signs of co-dependency and actively working to cultivate supportive behaviors empowers individuals to break free from unhealthy patterns. Building a strong foundation of trust, open communication, and mutual respect paves the way for a fulfilling partnership rooted in love and understanding.

Embracing the challenges of recovery together leads to deeper emotional connections. The process of healing and growth becomes a shared experience, fostering resilience in the relationship. As partners navigate the complexities of their individual journeys, they discover the beauty of supportive relationships that thrive on healthy dependency. The shift from co-dependency to supportive dynamics requires patience, but the rewards of a loving, balanced partnership far outweigh the challenges faced along the way. This journey encourages partners to become their best selves, supporting each other in recovery and beyond. The understanding of supportive versus co-dependent relationships serves as a guide for individuals seeking healthier connections in their lives.

Recognizing signs of co-dependency is vital for individuals seeking to establish and maintain healthy relationships, especially during the recovery process. Co-dependency often manifests subtly, making it challenging for individuals to identify its presence in their relationships. By understanding the indicators of co-dependent behavior, individuals can take proactive steps to break free from these patterns and foster healthier dynamics with their partners and loved ones.

One of the most prominent signs of co-dependency is an overwhelming sense of responsibility for another person's emotions and actions. If an individual feels compelled to manage their partner's feelings, constantly worrying about their happiness and well-being, this can be a red flag. Co-dependents often take on the emotional burden of their partner, leading to a skewed sense of responsibility. This behavior not only places undue pressure on the individual but also prevents their partner from taking ownership of their emotions, inhibiting personal growth for both parties. The partner reliant on the co-dependent individual may struggle to develop healthy coping mechanisms, perpetuating a cycle of emotional dependence.

Another significant indicator of co-dependency is the difficulty in asserting personal needs and boundaries. Individuals may prioritize their partner's needs above their own to the point of neglecting their well-being. This self-sacrificing behavior can manifest as agreeing to plans or compromising personal desires solely to avoid conflict or please their partner. Over time, this imbalance leads to feelings of resentment and frustration, as the individual suppresses their own needs for the sake of maintaining the relationship. Healthy relationships require open communication about needs and desires, and a lack of this communication may signify co-dependency.

Low self-esteem is often intertwined with co-dependent behaviors. Individuals may derive their sense of self-worth from their partner's validation, feeling incomplete or inadequate without their partner's approval. This reliance on external validation can lead to feelings of unworthiness and insecurity, causing individuals to feel trapped in a cycle of seeking approval and avoiding confrontation. Healthy self-esteem, on the other hand, allows individuals to appreciate themselves independently of their partner's perception. Recognizing and addressing self-esteem issues is crucial for breaking free from co-dependent patterns and fostering a healthier relationship dynamic.

Fear of abandonment frequently drives co-dependent behaviors. Individuals may go to great lengths to avoid conflict or dissatisfaction within the relationship, fearing that their partner will leave them if they express their true feelings. This fear can lead to unhealthy behaviors, such as people-pleasing, excessive apologizing, and emotional manipulation. It's essential to understand that while it's natural to have concerns about a relationship's stability, allowing fear to dictate behavior ultimately undermines the foundation of a healthy partnership. Establishing trust and open communication can help mitigate these fears and create a sense of security within the relationship.

Individuals entrenched in co-dependency often find themselves feeling trapped or overwhelmed in their relationships. They may experience feelings of being constantly drained or exhausted from the emotional labor involved in maintaining the relationship. This emotional exhaustion can stem from the relentless effort to manage their partner's feelings or the pressure to meet their needs at the expense of their own. Recognizing this feeling of being overwhelmed can serve as a wake-up call, prompting individuals to assess the health of their relationships and consider the toll it takes on their well-being.

Another sign of co-dependency is an inability to experience joy or fulfillment outside of the relationship. When individuals base their happiness solely on their partner's actions or emotions, they risk losing touch with their own interests, passions, and social circles. This loss of self can lead to isolation and disconnection from one's identity. Healthy relationships encourage partners to pursue their interests and support each other's personal growth. Recognizing the importance of individual happiness and fulfillment outside the partnership is crucial for fostering a balanced, supportive dynamic.

Co-dependency may also manifest as a pattern of enabling behaviors, particularly when one partner is struggling with addiction or emotional challenges. Enabling often includes making excuses for a partner's behavior, covering up their mistakes, or rescuing them from the consequences of their actions. This behavior may stem from a desire to protect the partner, but it ultimately hinders their personal growth and recovery. Enablers often feel conflicted, torn between their love for the partner and the desire to maintain peace within the relationship.

Recognizing these enabling behaviors is a critical step toward breaking the cycle of co-dependency and encouraging healthier dynamics.

Guilt and shame frequently accompany co-dependent relationships. Individuals may feel guilty for asserting their needs or desires, fearing it will upset their partner. They may also experience shame for not being able to "fix" their partner's problems or emotions. This guilt can create a vicious cycle, leading to self-sacrifice and a perpetuation of co-dependent patterns. It's essential for individuals to recognize that their needs are valid and that asserting them does not equate to selfishness. Overcoming guilt and shame requires reframing the narrative around self-worth and understanding that healthy relationships thrive on mutual respect and support.

The journey toward recognizing signs of co-dependency begins with self-reflection and awareness. Individuals should examine their behaviors, motivations, and emotional responses within their relationships. Journaling, therapy, and open conversations with trusted friends can provide valuable insights into relationship dynamics. As individuals become more aware of their patterns, they can take the necessary steps to break free from co-dependency and cultivate healthier, more supportive relationships.

Awareness of co-dependency serves as a crucial foundation for individuals seeking to establish and maintain healthy connections. Understanding these signs empowers individuals to take charge of their relationships and prioritize their well-being. By fostering open communication, setting boundaries, and practicing self-care, individuals can move toward healthier dynamics that promote mutual support and personal growth. Recognizing the distinction between supportive and co-dependent relationships enables individuals to forge connections that uplift and empower both partners, paving the way for a more fulfilling journey in recovery.

Building interdependent, balanced relationships is a fundamental aspect of personal growth and recovery. Interdependence fosters mutual respect, support, and healthy boundaries, allowing individuals to thrive both as individuals and as partners. Unlike co-dependency, which often leads to emotional exhaustion and a lack of personal identity, interdependence promotes a balanced dynamic where both partners contribute to each other's well-being without sacrificing their individuality.

At the heart of interdependence is the understanding that healthy relationships are based on mutual support rather than one-sided dependence. In an interdependent relationship, both partners recognize their individual strengths and weaknesses, understanding that they are both responsible for nurturing the connection. This means acknowledging each other's needs, desires, and emotions while also being accountable for one's own actions and responses. In recovery, where personal growth is paramount, cultivating interdependence can significantly enhance both partners' healing journeys.

Establishing trust is a crucial component of building interdependent relationships. Trust is built over time through consistent actions, open communication, and vulnerability. When both partners feel safe expressing their thoughts and emotions, they create an environment conducive to emotional intimacy. This openness allows for deeper connections, as both individuals can share their fears, dreams, and struggles without fear of judgment or rejection. Building trust requires ongoing effort, but the rewards are profound, leading to a stronger, more resilient partnership.

Communication plays a vital role in fostering interdependence. Healthy communication involves not only expressing one's needs and feelings but also actively listening to and validating the other person's perspective. When individuals feel heard and understood, it strengthens their connection and fosters a sense of belonging. In recovery, where emotions can be heightened, effective communication becomes even more critical. Partners should create a safe space for discussing difficult topics, setting aside time to check in with each other regularly. This practice not only enhances emotional intimacy but also helps to prevent misunderstandings and resentment from building up over time.

Another essential aspect of building interdependent relationships is the establishment of boundaries. Healthy boundaries allow individuals to maintain their sense of self while being supportive partners. Each person should communicate their boundaries clearly and respectfully, ensuring that both partners understand and respect these limits. Boundaries might include emotional boundaries, such as how much one is willing to share about their feelings, as well as physical boundaries regarding personal space and intimacy. By respecting each other's boundaries, individuals create a safe and supportive environment where both partners can flourish.

Interdependence also requires a balance of give and take. In a healthy partnership, both individuals contribute to the relationship in meaningful ways. This doesn't mean keeping score or measuring contributions but rather recognizing that relationships require effort from both parties. For instance, one partner might take on more responsibilities during a particularly challenging time, while the other may provide emotional support during a period of stress. Understanding that these dynamics may shift over time allows partners to adapt to each other's needs and create a harmonious balance within the relationship.

Furthermore, fostering interdependence involves supporting each other's individual growth. In recovery, personal development is vital, and partners should encourage one another to pursue their interests, hobbies, and goals. This support helps individuals maintain their identities outside the relationship, reducing the risk of losing themselves in the partnership. Celebrating each other's achievements, both big and small, reinforces a sense of teamwork and mutual respect. Encouraging personal growth ultimately enriches the relationship, as both partners can bring their unique experiences and perspectives to the partnership.

Developing healthy conflict resolution skills is another crucial aspect of interdependence. Conflicts are natural in any relationship, but how partners handle these disagreements can significantly impact the overall dynamic. Instead of resorting to blame or avoidance, interdependent partners approach conflict with empathy and a willingness to understand each other's viewpoints. This might involve taking a break during heated moments to cool down and reflect before revisiting the discussion with a calmer mindset. Learning to navigate conflict with compassion strengthens the relationship, reinforcing trust and emotional intimacy.

In addition to resolving conflicts, it's essential for partners to practice forgiveness. Holding onto grudges or past mistakes can hinder the growth of a relationship, leading to resentment and emotional distance. Interdependent relationships thrive on the ability to forgive and move forward together. This doesn't mean excusing harmful behaviors but rather acknowledging imperfections and allowing room for growth. When partners can forgive each other, they create a more resilient foundation that can withstand the challenges of recovery and life in general.

Recognizing the value of shared experiences can also enhance interdependence. Engaging in activities together—whether it's cooking a meal, going for walks, or participating in shared hobbies—can deepen emotional connections and create lasting memories. Shared experiences foster a sense of partnership and teamwork, reinforcing the idea that both individuals are invested in the relationship. It's important for partners to carve out quality time together, especially in recovery when life can become busy and overwhelming. This intentional time strengthens the bond and cultivates a shared sense of purpose.

As individuals progress in their recovery journey, it's crucial to remain aware of potential triggers that may impact their interdependent relationships. Life transitions, stressors, or unresolved emotional issues can surface, causing strain within the partnership. By maintaining open communication about these challenges, partners can navigate difficulties together, offering support and understanding. Being proactive in discussing triggers and coping strategies can prevent misunderstandings and allow for healthier responses to stress.

Ultimately, building interdependent, balanced relationships requires ongoing commitment and effort from both partners. It involves recognizing each other's needs, maintaining healthy communication, and supporting individual growth. By fostering trust, setting boundaries, and approaching conflict with empathy, individuals can create strong connections that uplift and empower both partners. Interdependence offers a powerful foundation for recovery, enabling individuals to thrive not only as individuals but also as partners committed to their shared journey.

Creating a healthy balance of independence and interdependence within a relationship requires intentional effort and practice. One essential exercise focuses on identifying personal interests and hobbies. Each partner should take time to explore activities that bring them joy and fulfillment, whether it's painting, hiking, or learning a new language. After this exploration, partners can share their interests with one another. Encouraging each other to pursue individual passions promotes a sense of autonomy and encourages growth outside the relationship, creating a foundation for interdependence.

Additionally, couples can practice setting boundaries that honor each individual's needs. An exercise involving boundary identification can help partners articulate what is acceptable and what is not within their relationship. This might include discussing personal space, emotional boundaries, and time for self-care. Writing these boundaries down and referring back to them can help partners remain accountable to each other, fostering respect and understanding.

Practicing self-reflection is another vital tool in cultivating independence. Each partner can engage in journaling to explore their thoughts, feelings, and experiences. This practice encourages personal growth and self-awareness, allowing individuals to understand their triggers, desires, and fears better. After a period of journaling, partners can share insights with each other, creating opportunities for deeper connection and empathy. This mutual sharing helps both partners recognize their individual journeys and supports the development of interdependence.

Mindfulness exercises can also play a significant role in building healthy dependency. Partners can engage in mindfulness practices together, such as meditation or yoga, that encourage presence and connection. These practices foster an environment where both individuals feel valued and understood, promoting emotional intimacy and trust. Engaging in these shared activities helps to create a sense of partnership and reinforces the idea that both individuals are committed to supporting each other's well-being.

Participating in community or support groups together is an excellent way to strengthen the bond of interdependence while respecting individual growth. This shared experience provides both partners with the opportunity to learn from others facing similar challenges. Attending these groups not only encourages personal growth but also reinforces the importance of mutual support in relationships. Through this process, couples can develop a deeper understanding of healthy interdependence.

Lastly, couples should establish rituals that promote connection while honoring individuality. These rituals might include regular date nights, cooking meals together, or taking turns planning weekend activities. Such practices help create shared memories and strengthen the bond between partners while allowing space for each individual to maintain their independence. By fostering a sense of togetherness while valuing personal space, partners can develop a balanced and supportive relationship.

In summary, cultivating independence and interdependence requires a variety of tools and practices. By engaging in goal-setting, boundary identification, self-reflection, mindfulness, and shared experiences, couples can foster a healthy balance that supports both personal growth and relationship stability. These practices lay the groundwork for a thriving partnership built on trust, understanding, and mutual respect.

Navigating the complexities of relationships in recovery is a multifaceted journey that demands patience, awareness, and continuous growth. Understanding the delicate balance between co-dependency and healthy dependency is essential for forging connections that are both supportive and nurturing. By recognizing the signs of co-dependency and actively working toward building interdependent relationships, individuals can create a solid foundation for lasting love and support. Through practical tools and exercises aimed at fostering independence and interdependence, couples can cultivate a relationship dynamic that honors their individual journeys while reinforcing their emotional bonds. Embracing these principles not only enhances personal well-being but also contributes to a more fulfilling and resilient partnership.

Chapter 10: Supporting Each Other's Recovery

Supporting a partner in recovery while ensuring you do not enable harmful behaviors is a delicate balance that requires awareness, compassion, and strong communication skills. Enabling occurs when one partner's actions inadvertently facilitate the other's addiction or unhealthy behaviors. This support, while well-intentioned, can undermine the progress both partners strive to achieve. Understanding the distinction between healthy support and enabling is vital for both partners' recovery journeys.

Recognizing enabling behaviors is the first step. Often, these actions stem from a desire to help, protect, or shield a partner from consequences. For instance, if a partner struggles with addiction and consistently misses work or responsibilities, stepping in to handle their obligations may seem like a gesture of love and support. However, this can allow them to avoid necessary consequences that could motivate change. Financial support is another area where enabling can occur. Providing money that can be used for substances or gambling, instead of focusing on recovery, reinforces dependency rather than promoting accountability.

Providing support without enabling requires a shift in perspective. Fostering an environment where a partner feels encouraged to take responsibility for their recovery is essential. Establishing boundaries plays a crucial role in this process. Boundaries define acceptable behavior and help maintain a healthy dynamic in the relationship. Communicating needs and limits openly is key. For example, expressing that while you want to be there for your partner during recovery, you cannot engage in activities or conversations that trigger their addiction is vital.

Creating a supportive environment includes being an active listener. Encourage your partner to express their feelings, struggles, and successes. Listening without judgment can help them feel validated and understood. Recovery often involves ups and downs, and showing patience and empathy during these moments is critical. Offer encouragement and remind your partner of their strengths while also encouraging them to seek help from professional support systems, such as therapy or support groups.

Engaging your partner through open-ended questions promotes reflection and growth. Instead of providing solutions, allow them to explore their thoughts and feelings. Asking, "What do you think triggered this setback?" encourages self-exploration rather than placing blame. This approach fosters a sense of agency, empowering your partner to take ownership of their recovery.

Practicing self-care remains essential when supporting a partner in recovery. The emotional toll of this journey can lead to burnout or resentment. Prioritizing your mental and physical health ensures resilience and capacity to offer support. Engaging in activities that bring joy, seeking out personal support systems, and considering counseling for yourself fosters overall well-being. Taking care of your needs equips you to provide the love and support your partner needs.

Celebrating milestones, no matter how small, reinforces positive behavior. Acknowledging progress instills motivation and encourages ongoing recovery. Celebrations don't have to be grand; simple acknowledgments, such as verbal praise or small treats, can make a significant impact. This recognition fosters a positive atmosphere where both partners feel valued and supported.

Providing accountability is a crucial aspect of support. While it's essential to be there for your partner, it's equally important to hold them accountable for their actions. Encourage responsibility by discussing consequences openly. For instance, if a partner engages in behaviors that jeopardize their recovery, calmly addressing the situation and discussing the potential impact can help them understand the importance of their choices.

Encouragement to seek professional help when necessary cannot be understated. Suggesting therapy or support groups as additional resources shows care for their recovery journey. Professional guidance can provide valuable tools for coping with challenges and developing healthier habits. Supporting your partner's decision to seek help strengthens the foundation of your relationship, fostering trust and understanding.

Involvement in your partner's recovery process is another way to show support without enabling. Attend support group meetings together or participate in family therapy. Engaging in these activities demonstrates commitment to their journey and helps build a shared understanding of the recovery process. This involvement can also create opportunities for open discussions about challenges and triumphs, further enhancing communication.

Encouraging independence is crucial for both partners' growth. Allowing your partner to navigate their recovery journey independently fosters confidence and resilience. Supporting their decision-making process, even when it leads to setbacks, teaches valuable lessons about responsibility and accountability. It's essential to recognize that recovery is not linear and that setbacks are a part of the process. Encouraging independence also involves refraining from taking over their responsibilities, allowing them to face challenges and grow from the experience.

Establishing a support network outside the relationship can be beneficial. Encourage your partner to connect with friends, family, or peers who support their recovery. This network provides additional emotional support and resources, lessening the burden on the relationship. Your partner's interactions with others can offer new perspectives and insights, contributing to their healing journey.

Developing a shared vision for the future strengthens the partnership. Discuss long-term goals, both individually and as a couple. This conversation fosters a sense of purpose and shared direction, encouraging both partners to work toward common objectives. Establishing this shared vision enhances motivation and reinforces commitment to recovery.

Incorporating fun and enjoyable activities into your relationship creates positive memories and strengthens the bond. Engaging in hobbies, going for walks, or cooking together can help shift focus away from the challenges of recovery, allowing both partners to enjoy quality time. These moments of joy can serve as a reminder of the love and support present in the relationship.

Honoring each other's boundaries is essential for maintaining a healthy relationship dynamic. Recognizing and respecting each other's limits fosters trust and communication. Discussing boundaries openly creates a safe space for both partners to express their needs and concerns, ultimately strengthening the relationship.

Support without enabling involves patience, understanding, and ongoing communication. It requires a commitment to fostering an environment where both partners feel valued and respected. Establishing boundaries, practicing self-care, celebrating milestones, and encouraging independence all contribute to a healthier partnership. By creating a supportive atmosphere, both partners can navigate the complexities of recovery together, emerging stronger and more resilient in their love for one another.

Encouraging a partner's growth in recovery involves fostering an environment that supports their personal journey while maintaining a balanced relationship. One essential aspect is understanding that recovery is an ongoing process filled with ups and downs. Partners should approach this journey with patience, recognizing that growth can take time and may not always follow a linear path. Encouragement starts with communication. Open and honest conversations about each other's goals, dreams, and fears create a foundation of trust and understanding. Partners can actively listen to one another's aspirations and validate their feelings, making it clear that their journey is taken seriously and appreciated.

Setting shared goals can be an effective way to encourage each other's growth. By creating mutual objectives, both partners work together toward a common purpose. These goals can be simple, such as attending a weekly support group together, or more ambitious, like planning a vacation that emphasizes sober activities. The key is to ensure these goals are realistic and achievable, allowing for small victories along the way. Celebrating these successes fosters a sense of accomplishment and reinforces the commitment to personal growth.

Providing emotional support plays a crucial role in this process. Being present for each other during difficult times strengthens the bond between partners. It's essential to acknowledge feelings of frustration or fear without judgment. Encouragement can manifest in simple gestures, like sending a text to check in or providing a comforting hug after a tough day. Showing empathy and understanding builds a solid support system, allowing both partners to feel valued and heard.

Understanding each partner's individual recovery journey is vital. While one partner may be focusing on developing new coping strategies, the other might be working on setting boundaries. It's crucial to respect each other's processes and avoid projecting personal timelines onto one another. Instead of offering unsolicited advice, partners can ask how they can help, providing space for dialogue about what kind of support is most beneficial. This approach allows each partner to feel empowered in their recovery journey.

Encouragement also extends to self-care practices. Reminding each other to prioritize self-care reinforces the idea that both partners deserve to focus on their mental and emotional health. Engaging in activities that promote wellness together, such as exercising, meditating, or even pursuing hobbies, not only encourages individual growth but also strengthens the relationship. Partners can explore new interests, deepening their connection while nurturing their personal development.

Setting boundaries around personal growth is equally important. While it's essential to encourage one another, partners must also recognize when to step back. Sometimes, the best way to support a partner's growth is to allow them the space to navigate challenges independently. This approach promotes self-reliance and self-discovery, both critical components of a healthy recovery. Encouraging independence while remaining available for support creates a balanced dynamic.

Conflict may arise during this journey, and how partners handle disagreements can significantly impact growth. Emphasizing healthy communication strategies during conflicts can transform potentially damaging situations into opportunities for growth. Practicing active listening, staying calm, and approaching discussions with compassion allows for constructive conversations. It's essential to focus on the issue rather than resorting to personal attacks. When disagreements occur, partners should work together to find solutions that respect both individuals' needs.

Creating an environment where both partners can express their feelings without fear of judgment fosters openness and trust. Regular check-ins can help maintain this atmosphere, providing a designated time for partners to discuss their emotional states, concerns, or progress. These conversations can strengthen the connection between partners, reinforcing their commitment to supporting one another's growth.

Encouragement can also come from seeking outside support. Attending couples' therapy or participating in support groups designed for partners of individuals in recovery can provide valuable insights and tools for growth. These resources offer an opportunity to learn from others' experiences, share challenges, and discover new strategies for supporting one another effectively.

Understanding the power of positive reinforcement can significantly impact a partner's growth. Recognizing and celebrating milestones, no matter how small, helps create a culture of encouragement. Simple acknowledgments, such as saying, "I'm proud of you for reaching out for help" or "You handled that situation really well," can boost self-esteem and motivate continued progress. Positive reinforcement reinforces the behaviors and changes partners want to see, cultivating an environment conducive to growth.

Finally, embracing vulnerability in the relationship can foster deeper connections. Sharing fears, struggles, and aspirations allows partners to understand each other on a more profound level. This openness can break down walls, promoting trust and intimacy essential for a thriving relationship. By creating a safe space where vulnerability is welcomed, partners encourage each other to be authentic and genuine in their recovery journeys.

Encouraging a partner's growth requires ongoing commitment and active participation from both individuals. Communication, emotional support, shared goals, and mutual respect create a foundation that fosters personal development. Recognizing the unique challenges of recovery while celebrating successes strengthens the bond between partners. Emphasizing self-care, setting boundaries, and navigating conflicts with compassion further enhances the relationship's resilience. In this journey of growth, partners can cultivate a partnership that not only supports recovery but also thrives on love, trust, and mutual understanding.

Dealing with relapses and setbacks is an inevitable part of the recovery journey. While every individual hopes for a smooth path toward sobriety, reality often presents challenges that can test even the strongest commitment. A crucial aspect of supporting a partner during these difficult moments is understanding that relapse does not signify failure but rather a signal that further growth is needed. Partners must approach these situations with empathy and compassion, recognizing that setbacks can occur for a variety of reasons, including stress, unresolved emotions, or external pressures.

Creating a safe space for open discussions about relapse is essential. Partners should establish an environment where feelings can be shared without fear of judgment or shame. By discussing fears and triggers, partners can better understand what led to the relapse and develop strategies to address those challenges in the future. It's vital for both individuals to express their emotions and fears, allowing for a deeper understanding of the underlying issues contributing to the setback.

Recognizing that relapse often brings feelings of guilt and shame is crucial. Partners must be aware of these emotions and work together to navigate through them. Instead of placing blame, it is more productive to focus on understanding the circumstances surrounding the relapse. Encouraging honest conversations about feelings of guilt can help alleviate the emotional burden and promote healing. By framing the experience as a learning opportunity rather than a failure, partners can help each other regain motivation and confidence.

Developing a relapse prevention plan can be beneficial for both partners. This plan should include specific strategies to identify triggers, coping mechanisms to deal with cravings, and support resources available during challenging times. By collaborating on this plan, partners can feel more invested in each other's recovery journeys. Regularly reviewing and updating the plan as needed allows both partners to remain proactive and engaged in their recovery processes.

It's also essential to address the stigma surrounding relapse. Many individuals in recovery feel isolated after a setback, believing that they have disappointed their loved ones. Partners should work together to dispel these feelings by reinforcing the idea that recovery is a journey filled with ups and downs. Sharing stories of other individuals who have faced similar challenges can help normalize the experience and offer hope for a successful recovery.

Encouragement is paramount during times of relapse. Partners should remind each other of their strengths and the progress they have made thus far. This reinforcement can help rebuild self-esteem and confidence. Verbal affirmations, such as "You've overcome so much already, and I believe in you," can be powerful motivators. Partners can also celebrate small victories in the recovery process, reinforcing the notion that every step forward counts.

In addition to emotional support, practical strategies can help both partners navigate relapses effectively. Identifying specific triggers, such as particular situations or environments, can aid in avoiding relapse risks in the future. Keeping a journal to track feelings and experiences during difficult times can provide insights into patterns that may need to be addressed. This reflective practice can help partners develop a deeper understanding of their emotional responses, equipping them with the tools to handle similar situations moving forward.

Encouraging participation in support groups, either individually or as a couple, can also provide valuable resources during times of relapse. These groups often offer a sense of community and shared understanding, fostering connections with others who have faced similar challenges. Hearing others share their experiences can be uplifting, reminding partners that they are not alone in their struggles. Seeking professional help, such as therapy or counseling, can provide additional guidance in navigating the complexities of relapse.

In moments of crisis, practicing self-care is vital for both partners. Each person must prioritize their mental and emotional well-being, as stress can compound the challenges associated with relapse. Engaging in activities that promote relaxation, such as exercise, meditation, or spending time in nature, can help both partners maintain their balance and perspective. Taking time for oneself can prevent burnout and promote resilience, allowing each individual to offer more support to their partner during difficult times.

Understanding the importance of boundaries during relapses is also crucial. Partners should establish clear boundaries to protect their emotional health while offering support. This balance can prevent co-dependency, ensuring that each person maintains their individual identity and well-being. Recognizing when to step back and encourage independence can empower the partner in recovery, fostering self-reliance and personal growth.

Communication remains a cornerstone of navigating relapses. Partners should continuously check in with each other, discussing how they are feeling and what support is needed. Creating a regular dialogue allows both individuals to remain engaged in the recovery process, reinforcing their commitment to one another. Being attentive to each other's needs fosters a deeper connection, allowing both partners to feel heard and understood.

As the recovery journey progresses, partners should remember that setbacks are not indicative of their overall progress. Each relapse can serve as a catalyst for growth and learning. By approaching these challenges with patience and compassion, partners can strengthen their bond and develop a deeper understanding of each other's journeys. Emphasizing the importance of support, open communication, and self-care fosters resilience in the relationship. Together, they can navigate the complexities of recovery, emerging stronger and more united in their commitment to sobriety.

In supporting each other's recovery, practical tools play a crucial role in navigating the complexities of addiction and maintaining a healthy relationship. Establishing accountability practices is one of the most effective ways to create an environment conducive to sobriety and personal growth. Regular check-ins can be a powerful tool for both partners, providing a safe space to share feelings, struggles, and successes. This practice not only fosters open communication but also reinforces accountability, ensuring both individuals remain committed to their recovery journeys. By sharing their experiences, partners can offer each other support and encouragement, creating a sense of teamwork that is essential for lasting recovery.

Setting measurable and achievable goals becomes a cornerstone of accountability practices. Partners should openly discuss their individual recovery objectives and strategize on how to support one another in reaching those goals. For example, if one partner aims to attend more support meetings, the other can offer to join them or help facilitate discussions about their experiences. Celebrating progress, regardless of its size, is equally important. Recognizing and acknowledging each other's milestones fosters motivation and reinforces positive behaviors associated with sobriety, creating an environment where both partners feel valued and supported.

Developing a relapse response plan is another practical tool that can significantly aid both partners in their recovery journey. This plan acts as a safety net, providing a clear strategy for what to do if a relapse occurs. By creating this plan together, partners can ensure they are on the same page regarding how to handle potential crises. This proactive approach not only reduces anxiety during difficult times but also creates a sense of security within the relationship. The relapse response plan should identify specific triggers, coping strategies, and available resources for support. For instance, if stress is a known trigger, the plan might include techniques such as deep breathing exercises or contacting a therapist or support group for immediate assistance.

Incorporating support resources into the relapse response plan is essential. Both partners should compile a list of contacts to reach out to during challenging moments. This list can include friends, family members, therapists, or support groups, allowing partners to combat feelings of isolation and seek help when needed. Knowing when to involve professional assistance is another critical component of the plan. If a relapse occurs and emotions become overwhelming, recognizing the need for a therapist or counselor can be a crucial lifeline.

Journaling serves as another valuable practice that enhances accountability and self-reflection. Each partner can maintain a personal journal to document their emotions, triggers, and reactions to various challenges. This practice fosters greater self-awareness, allowing individuals to identify patterns or recurring issues that may need addressing. Sharing journal entries can facilitate deeper conversations, promoting understanding and empathy within the relationship.

Affirmation practices also hold significant potential in recovery. Partners can engage in daily or weekly affirmations that resonate with them, reinforcing their commitment to sobriety. These positive reminders serve to uplift both individuals, reminding them of their strengths and shared goals. Supporting each other in this practice fosters a collective sense of motivation and hope, deepening the bond between partners.

Incorporating mindfulness practices into daily routines can greatly enhance recovery efforts. Techniques such as meditation, deep breathing, or yoga can help both partners remain grounded during challenging times. Engaging in these practices together fosters a sense of connection and unity in their recovery journeys. Prioritizing mindfulness equips partners to manage stress more effectively, reducing the likelihood of relapse and encouraging a healthy relationship dynamic.

Maintaining balance within the relationship is essential as both partners engage in recovery. While accountability and support are vital, prioritizing self-care is equally important. Establishing personal boundaries ensures that individual well-being remains a top priority. Encouraging each other to engage in hobbies, exercise, or activities that bring joy contributes to overall mental and emotional health. This balance prevents either partner from becoming overly reliant on the other for emotional support, promoting a healthier form of interdependence.

The importance of ongoing communication cannot be overstated as the chapter nears its conclusion. Regular discussions about the effectiveness of established accountability practices and the relapse response plan are vital for continuous improvement. Both partners should feel comfortable expressing their thoughts on what is working and what might need adjustment. This ongoing dialogue fosters flexibility and adaptation, ensuring the tools remain relevant and effective in the recovery process.

Establishing accountability practices and developing a relapse response plan are crucial steps in supporting each partner's recovery journey. By working together, partners can create an environment rooted in trust, understanding, and resilience. The practical tools discussed in this chapter provide strategies for navigating the complexities of recovery, reinforcing the idea that setbacks do not define the journey but rather serve as opportunities for growth and learning. Through open communication, mutual support, and proactive planning, couples can strengthen their bond and emerge from challenges with renewed commitment to their sobriety and relationship.

Chapter 11: Creating New, Shared Memories

Creating new memories is a vital aspect of recovery that can strengthen the bond between partners. New experiences foster growth, build resilience, and promote a sense of joy, which is essential for both individual and relational healing. Engaging in activities together allows couples to break away from the patterns established during addiction, paving the way for healthier dynamics. The shared joy of new experiences cultivates intimacy and trust, essential components in rebuilding a relationship that may have been strained or damaged by addiction. Establishing these new memories is not only about creating moments of happiness; it's also about learning to enjoy life together again, discovering shared interests, and fostering a renewed sense of purpose.

Experiencing life through a fresh lens can help partners redefine their relationship. In recovery, individuals often discover aspects of themselves that were previously overshadowed by addiction. As partners embark on this journey together, they can explore these new facets, encouraging one another to step outside their comfort zones and embrace unfamiliar situations. This exploration can lead to significant personal growth, allowing each individual to develop a deeper understanding of themselves and each other. Creating new memories together provides a unique opportunity to witness each other's evolution, enhancing appreciation and admiration for one another.

New experiences also contribute to breaking the cycle of negative patterns that may have developed during active addiction. Engaging in activities that foster joy and connection can counterbalance the hardships faced during the recovery process. Whether it's hiking in nature, cooking a new recipe together, or traveling to a new destination, these experiences can inject vitality into a relationship that may have felt stagnant or defined by past struggles. They serve as reminders that life can be enjoyable, and they can help partners to redefine what happiness looks like in their lives moving forward.

Shared experiences can act as a form of therapy, providing an avenue for healing and discussion. When partners engage in activities that challenge them or push them to confront their fears, it opens the door for deeper conversations about their experiences, emotions, and struggles. This vulnerability is crucial for building a strong foundation in recovery relationships. By navigating new experiences together, partners can create a safe space for discussing their fears, hopes, and aspirations. This dialogue not only fosters understanding but also cultivates empathy, reinforcing the bond between partners.

Celebrating milestones through new experiences can also be a significant aspect of recovery. Whether it's celebrating sobriety anniversaries or personal achievements, finding ways to mark these moments can be powerful. Doing something special to commemorate these milestones allows couples to honor their journey and recognize the hard work that goes into maintaining recovery. This celebration reinforces the idea that recovery is a shared journey and that each partner plays a vital role in supporting the other's growth.

Trying new things together also encourages open-mindedness and adaptability. In recovery, flexibility becomes a vital skill as individuals learn to navigate life's ups and downs. By embracing new experiences, partners can develop a shared sense of adventure, fostering resilience that can be beneficial in facing future challenges. This adaptability strengthens the relationship, equipping both partners with the tools to manage stressors in a healthier way.

Exploring new hobbies or interests can serve as a foundation for building new memories. Couples might consider taking a class together, such as painting, dancing, or cooking. These activities not only provide a fun outlet but also create opportunities for bonding and teamwork. Working together toward a common goal encourages communication and collaboration, essential elements for nurturing a healthy relationship. Through these shared experiences, partners learn to appreciate each other's strengths and support each other in areas where they might struggle.

Traveling can be an incredibly enriching experience for couples in recovery. Whether it's a weekend getaway or a longer vacation, getting away from the routine can refresh perspectives and ignite creativity. Traveling together allows couples to create lasting memories that are entirely separate from their past experiences. Exploring new places can also foster a sense of adventure, encouraging spontaneity and excitement. This shared adventure can lead to new insights about each other, deepening the connection and understanding within the relationship.

It's important to recognize that new experiences don't always need to be grand or extravagant. Simple activities like going for a walk, visiting a local museum, or trying a new restaurant can be just as meaningful. The focus should be on creating moments of connection and joy, no matter how big or small. These shared experiences contribute to the overall quality of the relationship, reinforcing the idea that recovery is not just about sobriety but about enriching life together.

Incorporating elements of fun and playfulness into the relationship can also be therapeutic. Allowing space for laughter and lightheartedness helps to alleviate some of the pressures associated with recovery. This playfulness can manifest in various ways, such as playful banter, games, or impromptu adventures. Creating an environment where both partners feel free to express joy and spontaneity fosters a healthy dynamic that encourages resilience and healing.

As partners invest in creating new, shared memories, they begin to establish a narrative that is distinctly their own, separate from the challenges of addiction. This new narrative can be empowering, providing both partners with a sense of agency and control over their lives. Instead of feeling defined by their past, couples can cultivate a future filled with hope, joy, and possibility.

Engaging in healthy, enjoyable activities together plays a crucial role in nurturing relationships in recovery. These activities not only foster connection but also promote well-being, providing couples with the opportunity to bond over shared experiences. Finding the right activities that both partners enjoy can be a delightful journey in itself. Exploring various options helps each individual discover new interests while strengthening their relationship. Activities that promote physical health, emotional connection, and shared enjoyment can enhance the overall quality of a partnership.

One of the simplest yet most effective activities is to engage in outdoor adventures. Nature offers a healing backdrop that can rejuvenate the spirit. Couples can explore local parks, hiking trails, or beaches, allowing the beauty of the natural world to enhance their time together. Hiking, in particular, provides not only physical benefits but also the opportunity to have deep conversations while navigating the trails. Sharing the experience of reaching a summit or discovering a beautiful view can create lasting memories and reinforce the idea of teamwork in a relationship.

Cooking together is another enjoyable activity that can strengthen bonds. It offers an opportunity to collaborate, communicate, and explore creativity. Preparing meals can be a fun way to experiment with new ingredients and recipes, allowing partners to share their preferences and culinary skills. Cooking can also promote healthy eating habits, which are vital in recovery. Preparing nutritious meals together cultivates a sense of accomplishment, while sharing the fruits of that labor can create intimate moments around the dining table. Furthermore, this activity can lead to new traditions, such as themed dinners or cooking nights, enhancing the couple's shared experiences.

Exploring the world of arts and crafts can provide a therapeutic outlet for couples. Engaging in creative activities such as painting, pottery, or crafting allows partners to express themselves and their emotions in a unique way. This process of creating art together can foster open communication and provide insights into each other's feelings and experiences. It is a wonderful opportunity to share vulnerabilities and enjoy the satisfaction of creating something beautiful together. The act of collaborating on a project can serve as a metaphor for the relationship, illustrating how two individuals can come together to create something meaningful.

Participating in volunteer work can also be a rewarding activity that strengthens the relationship. Giving back to the community fosters a sense of purpose and connection, as partners work together toward a common goal. Whether it's serving meals at a shelter, participating in a local cleanup, or supporting a charity event, volunteering creates opportunities for meaningful conversations and shared experiences. This type of activity reinforces the idea that recovery is not just about individual healing; it's also about contributing positively to the world around them. The satisfaction of helping others can also bolster self-esteem and create a sense of fulfillment in both partners.

Taking up a new sport or physical activity together can be an exhilarating way to bond. Whether it's joining a local gym, participating in yoga classes, or trying out a new sport like tennis or rock climbing, engaging in physical activities encourages teamwork and accountability. Fitness challenges or goals can also be set, allowing couples to motivate one another and celebrate achievements together. This shared commitment to health fosters a deeper sense of partnership, as both individuals support each other in their journeys toward improved well-being.

Traveling together, even if it's just a day trip to a nearby town, can create lasting memories and deepen the relationship. Exploring new places provides a break from the routine, introducing excitement and novelty.

Couples can plan trips that involve activities they both enjoy, whether it's visiting historical sites, enjoying local cuisine, or participating in outdoor adventures. These shared experiences allow partners to bond over new adventures and create a collective narrative that strengthens their connection.

Reading together can be an enriching experience, allowing partners to explore new ideas and perspectives. Choosing a book to read together, whether it's fiction, non-fiction, or self-help, opens the door for meaningful discussions. After finishing a chapter or a book, partners can engage in conversations about the themes, characters, and lessons learned, deepening their understanding of each other's viewpoints. This activity promotes intellectual intimacy and encourages partners to share their thoughts and feelings in a supportive environment.

Attending workshops or classes together can also be a great way to strengthen a relationship. Whether it's a dance class, a writing workshop, or a seminar on personal development, these shared learning experiences can foster growth and connection. Partners can encourage each other to step out of their comfort zones, supporting one another in new challenges. The shared journey of learning can lead to new insights about each other and strengthen the bond as partners work together toward personal development.

Mindfulness practices, such as meditation or yoga, can be incredibly beneficial for couples in recovery. Practicing mindfulness together fosters emotional connection, promotes stress reduction, and enhances communication. These activities encourage partners to be present with one another, fostering a deeper understanding of their feelings and experiences. Sharing mindfulness practices can lead to greater empathy and compassion in the relationship, as both partners learn to navigate their emotional landscapes together.

Creating a shared bucket list can be an exciting way for couples to envision their future together. Writing down dreams, aspirations, and activities they want to experience can serve as a motivating reminder of what they're working toward in their recovery journey. Regularly revisiting this list allows partners to check off completed items and add new ones as they discover new interests. This shared vision can foster hope and excitement about the future, reinforcing the idea that they are building a life together beyond addiction.

Ultimately, finding enjoyable activities that resonate with both partners is essential for nurturing a healthy, supportive relationship. By exploring new hobbies, engaging in shared experiences, and fostering creativity, couples in recovery can deepen their connection and create meaningful memories. These activities serve as a reminder that life can be fulfilling and joyful, reinforcing the idea that recovery is not solely about overcoming challenges but also about embracing new opportunities for happiness. Creating new, shared memories can transform a relationship, providing a solid foundation for a bright, shared future together.

Celebrating milestones in recovery as a couple is a powerful way to acknowledge progress, strengthen bonds, and cultivate a shared sense of accomplishment. These milestones can range from sobriety anniversaries to personal achievements in self-development and emotional growth. Recognizing these moments together not only honors the hard work each partner has put into their recovery journey but also reinforces the commitment to support one another as they navigate the challenges of sobriety.

Acknowledging sobriety anniversaries is an essential part of celebrating recovery. These dates mark significant progress and serve as reminders of the resilience and strength both partners have shown. Celebrating these anniversaries can take various forms, from hosting a small gathering with supportive friends and family to enjoying a special dinner together. Creating rituals around these dates can make them more meaningful, such as writing letters to each other that reflect on the past year, sharing hopes for the future, and expressing gratitude for the support provided. These rituals can help partners reconnect with their individual journeys and recognize the importance of their collective efforts.

Personal achievements, whether in career, education, or personal goals, also deserve to be celebrated. Recognizing these accomplishments fosters a sense of pride and validation for both partners. For example, if one partner completes a course or achieves a work-related goal, the other can plan a special outing or surprise celebration to honor that effort. This acknowledgment shows that each partner is invested in the other's growth and success, reinforcing the idea that they are a team working toward mutual aspirations. Celebrating these milestones can strengthen emotional connections, providing opportunities for partners to express their admiration and appreciation for each other's accomplishments.

In addition to sobriety anniversaries and personal achievements, it's important to celebrate smaller, everyday victories. Recovery is filled with numerous challenges, and acknowledging the little wins can boost morale and motivation. Whether it's sticking to a routine, managing stress effectively, or practicing healthy coping strategies, celebrating these small victories can have a profound impact on both partners. Taking time to recognize and celebrate these moments creates a culture of positivity and support within the relationship. It reinforces the idea that progress is a continuous journey, and every step forward deserves recognition.

Celebrating milestones can also include setting and achieving shared goals as a couple. Establishing mutual aspirations fosters teamwork and collaboration, allowing both partners to contribute their ideas and efforts. Whether it's planning a trip together, starting a new hobby, or creating a shared project, working toward common goals can strengthen the relationship. Celebrating the completion of these goals not only brings joy but also deepens the sense of partnership. For instance, if a couple decides to participate in a charity run together, crossing the finish line can be a monumental moment worth celebrating. Recognizing their teamwork in achieving a shared goal reinforces the notion that they are stronger together.

Creative expression can be a meaningful way to celebrate milestones in recovery. Engaging in activities that allow partners to express their feelings can deepen emotional connections. For example, couples might choose to create a scrapbook that highlights their recovery journey, documenting important milestones, photos, and reflections. This creative project becomes a tangible reminder of their progress, providing both partners with a sense of ownership over their narrative. Additionally, exploring artistic pursuits, such as painting or writing, can serve as a therapeutic outlet for emotions tied to their recovery experiences. Celebrating through creativity fosters connection while allowing both partners to process their feelings in a constructive way.

Embracing traditions around milestones can also enhance the significance of these celebrations. For example, couples might develop a yearly tradition of visiting a special location that holds meaning for them, such as the place where they first met or a location that symbolizes their journey. Creating new traditions that revolve around their recovery milestones reinforces a sense of unity and shared identity. These traditions can provide a sense of stability and continuity, reminding both partners of the progress they've made and the future they are building together. By celebrating in ways that resonate personally, couples can create lasting memories that become part of their unique recovery story.

Incorporating elements of gratitude into milestone celebrations can enhance their impact. Taking a moment to express appreciation for one another during these special occasions fosters a culture of gratitude within the relationship. Each partner can reflect on the role the other has played in their recovery journey and acknowledge the sacrifices and efforts made. This practice not only strengthens emotional bonds but also promotes a sense of shared responsibility for each other's well-being. Gratitude can transform the way partners view their relationship, reinforcing the idea that they are both active participants in each other's growth.

It's essential to recognize that not all milestones will be monumental. Some may be quieter, more subtle moments of progress that deserve attention. For instance, the day one partner feels confident enough to attend a social event without using substances can be a milestone worth celebrating. Recognizing these seemingly small achievements reinforces the idea that recovery is a holistic journey. Each moment of progress contributes to the overall narrative of healing, and acknowledging these moments allows couples to cultivate a deeper appreciation for their journey.

As couples navigate their recovery journeys together, celebrating milestones fosters connection, promotes emotional intimacy, and strengthens their partnership. These celebrations serve as reminders of the resilience and determination required to overcome challenges, reinforcing the belief that recovery is possible. By creating meaningful traditions, acknowledging achievements, and incorporating gratitude, couples can cultivate a supportive environment where both partners thrive. Celebrating milestones together not only honors the past but also paves the way for a brighter future, filled with shared experiences, love, and continued growth. Ultimately, these celebrations are an affirmation of their commitment to one another and their collective journey of healing.

Creating a couple's bucket list strengthens the relationship and fosters a sense of adventure and excitement within recovery. This shared list serves as a tangible reminder of the experiences both partners wish to pursue together, emphasizing the importance of building positive memories as they navigate their recovery journey. When creating a bucket list, encouraging open communication about each partner's dreams, aspirations, and interests is essential. This collaborative process not only helps partners learn more about each other but also cultivates a deeper emotional connection. Couples can start by brainstorming ideas that reflect their shared values and individual passions. This may include travel destinations, activities they want to try together, or personal goals they wish to achieve. Once they have compiled a list of potential experiences, partners should prioritize these goals based on their interests and feasibility. It's important to consider both short-term and long-term goals, ensuring a balance between achievable tasks and more ambitious dreams. For instance, they might decide to plan a weekend getaway to a nearby city while also including a dream of visiting an international destination in the future. Having a mix of both allows for immediate gratification and long-term excitement, reinforcing the idea that they are working together toward fulfilling their aspirations.

Celebrating milestones in recovery doesn't just end with recognizing sobriety anniversaries; it can also encompass celebrating personal achievements, relationship growth, and new experiences together. When planning milestone celebrations, couples can reflect on what accomplishments they want to honor, whether that be a significant step in their recovery journey or a meaningful moment in their relationship. This process helps partners acknowledge their progress and reinforces the idea that their efforts are worth celebrating. Creating unique rituals for milestone celebrations adds a layer of significance to these moments. Couples can establish traditions that resonate with them, such as a yearly dinner where they share reflections on their journey, express gratitude for each other, and discuss future goals. These rituals provide opportunities for connection and can deepen emotional intimacy. Additionally, they can explore fun and creative ways to celebrate, such as creating a scrapbook or a video montage that captures their milestones, helping to visualize their journey and the experiences they've shared. Moreover, incorporating elements of surprise into milestone celebrations can enhance the excitement and joy. One partner can plan a surprise celebration for the other, showing appreciation and thoughtfulness that reinforces the bond between them. This act of kindness fosters a supportive atmosphere, reminding both partners of the importance of celebrating not just major milestones but also the smaller, meaningful moments that contribute to their recovery.

To make these celebrations even more impactful, couples can involve supportive friends or family members who understand their journey. Sharing milestones with loved ones provides a sense of community and support that can strengthen their recovery. Friends and family can participate in the celebrations, whether through organizing a gathering or simply sending messages of encouragement. This inclusiveness reinforces the idea that recovery is a journey best traveled with others, and the support of a broader community can be invaluable. In addition to creating a couple's bucket list and establishing milestone celebration traditions, practical tools like journaling can serve as a valuable resource for couples in recovery. Maintaining a shared journal where both partners can document their thoughts, feelings, and reflections about their journey together can promote emotional intimacy and transparency. This practice allows each partner to express themselves freely and facilitates open conversations about their experiences, challenges, and victories. By reviewing their journal entries during milestone celebrations, couples can reflect on how far they've come and reaffirm their commitment to supporting each other in recovery.

Incorporating these practical tools into their recovery journey helps couples create a positive, growth-oriented environment. By actively engaging in experiences that align with their shared goals, acknowledging their milestones, and celebrating both personal and relationship achievements, partners can strengthen their bond and cultivate a fulfilling life together. Each celebration, adventure, and shared aspiration becomes a testament to their resilience and love, serving as a reminder that they are not alone in their journey and that every step taken together contributes to a brighter future.

Now you know that creating new, shared memories plays a crucial role in recovery relationships, serving as a foundation for stronger emotional connections between partners. New experiences provide couples with opportunities to bond and grow together in a healthy manner. Engaging in enjoyable activities not only strengthens their relationship but also offers essential support during challenging times in their recovery journey. Celebrating milestones, whether related to sobriety or personal growth, allows couples to acknowledge their progress and accomplishments, fostering a sense of shared pride and unity. Establishing meaningful traditions around these celebrations can enhance their connection and provide lasting memories that reinforce their commitment to one another. Involving supportive friends and family creates a broader community that uplifts both partners during their recovery, enriching their shared experiences. Practical tools, such as a couple's bucket list and shared journaling, empower couples to intentionally cultivate these moments and reflect on their journey together. These practices foster a positive environment that nurtures love, understanding, and resilience.

Chapter 12: Overcoming Challenges Together

When obstacles emerge in recovery, they can feel overwhelming, especially when familiar, unproductive patterns threaten to resurface. Whether the pattern is avoidance, withdrawal, or reacting defensively, recognizing these old responses can be the first step in moving past them. Recovery brings its own set of challenges, and in a relationship, the dynamic can magnify them. Facing obstacles together requires patience, new perspectives, and the ability to embrace healthier responses over comfortable but ultimately self-defeating habits.

In early recovery, many people find that they naturally gravitate toward familiar behaviors when confronted with stress. In these moments, it's easy to return to the paths we know—ones shaped by past coping mechanisms that often led to dysfunction. However, these patterns no longer serve us, and their return can undermine the hard work put into building a new life. Recognizing these tendencies as they arise provides a chance to choose a different path, one grounded in resilience and shared growth rather than reaction.

Facing challenges together calls for a level of transparency that might feel uncomfortable initially. Being open about fears, setbacks, or insecurities creates a safe environment for growth. Recovery itself thrives in openness, and when each partner can trust that they can share without fear of judgment or rejection, a stronger foundation is built. Talking openly about triggers and vulnerabilities isn't a sign of weakness; it's a courageous step toward understanding and support. Establishing this transparency as a standard in the relationship allows both partners to feel secure, even during moments of tension.

Releasing old habits also means stepping into unfamiliar methods of problem-solving. In place of avoidance, a couple might practice addressing challenges directly, even if it feels awkward at first. Instead of falling into blame cycles, they can develop a habit of viewing each situation through a lens of shared accountability and understanding. Active listening—a practice of truly hearing the other person's words, feelings, and needs—can replace defensive responses. Listening actively not only validates each partner's experiences but also creates a sense of unity and shared purpose.

Learning to pause during heated moments can be transformative. A pause allows each person a moment to breathe, reflect, and choose their response consciously rather than reflexively. The power of a well-timed pause helps to shift conversations from reaction to response, encouraging calmness and thoughtfulness. Pausing may be as simple as taking a few deep breaths or as deliberate as agreeing to revisit the discussion after emotions have settled. This habit doesn't erase conflict but allows for more constructive, respectful engagement.

Establishing healthy boundaries is critical when navigating obstacles without slipping back into unhelpful patterns. Each partner must be mindful of their own limits and communicate them clearly. Boundaries protect the space each individual needs to grow while preserving the relationship's integrity. They act as a safety net, ensuring that both partners feel respected and valued. Effective boundary-setting also involves respecting the boundaries of the other person, recognizing that each individual's needs may differ and may even change over time. When past habits threaten to emerge, it helps to rely on new coping strategies that foster resilience. Practicing mindfulness, whether through meditation, journaling, or simply being present, allows each partner to ground themselves in the present rather than being pulled into past behaviors. These techniques help both individuals become aware of their emotional triggers and patterns, offering them a chance to choose different reactions. Engaging in these practices together creates a shared sense of calm and connection, a reminder that they are a team navigating recovery side by side.

A focus on problem-solving rather than blame sets a positive tone during difficult times. Instead of falling into patterns of pointing fingers, a solution-oriented mindset helps both partners to work collaboratively. Phrasing concerns as "we" rather than "you" or "me" statements emphasizes the partnership and reduces defensiveness. In this way, challenges become shared experiences rather than sources of division, helping the relationship grow stronger through adversity.

Regular reflection on personal and shared progress is crucial. In recovery, both individuals may face moments of self-doubt or frustration, especially when it feels like obstacles are unrelenting. Taking time to acknowledge small victories—whether in managing emotions, making healthier choices, or supporting one another—reinforces each partner's commitment to recovery and to each other. It's easy to lose sight of progress when difficulties arise, but looking back on the journey as a whole can provide reassurance and motivation to continue forward.

Turning to a supportive community can make a significant difference. Sometimes, overcoming challenges requires outside perspectives and advice. Support groups, therapy, or simply connecting with friends who understand recovery can provide valuable insights. Involving others can prevent isolation and offer encouragement, as well as a reminder that no one has to face obstacles alone. The wisdom and experiences of others in similar situations can bring fresh perspectives that enrich the relationship.

Choosing not to rely on old patterns ultimately comes down to creating a relationship built on trust, respect, and open communication. When both partners are committed to personal growth, they naturally support each other's progress. As challenges arise, a focus on shared solutions over individual reactions shifts the relationship from one that is reactive to one that is resilient. A partnership in recovery becomes a space of healing and mutual empowerment, where both individuals are free to be themselves and grow together.

In moments of struggle, it's helpful to remind each other of the strength that brought them to this point. Reflecting on past accomplishments in recovery, even those that seem small, fosters hope and confidence. The journey isn't about avoiding difficulty but about learning to face it with patience, compassion, and integrity. Embracing these values, couples can look forward to a future where obstacles are not threats but opportunities for deeper connection and growth. This mutual commitment to overcoming challenges allows the relationship to thrive beyond the patterns of the past, laying a foundation for a healthier and more fulfilling partnership.

Handling stress, financial strain, and the inevitable transitions in sobriety demands a blend of resilience, adaptability, and patience. Life's challenges don't stop after recovery begins—instead, they often reveal themselves in new and unexpected ways. Each new transition, whether it's returning to work, rebuilding finances, or facing daily stressors, offers its own unique test of a couple's commitment to each other and to their recovery journey. For couples working toward a life of sobriety, learning to face these pressures together can foster growth and unity, turning difficult times into meaningful progress rather than setbacks.

Stress comes in various forms in early recovery and can stem from routine situations that may not have seemed challenging before. Even simple decisions can feel weighty under the lens of recovery, with each choice potentially impacting both sobriety and the relationship. This heightened sensitivity is common and completely normal. The goal, however, isn't to avoid stress altogether but to learn healthier ways of handling it. Taking a proactive approach to stress management—by setting aside regular times for open communication, daily check-ins, or establishing unwinding routines—creates a buffer against moments when tension could otherwise disrupt harmony.

Financial strain often becomes a significant hurdle, especially if previous addiction led to financial losses or instability. Recovery itself can be costly, with expenses such as therapy, support groups, and healthcare. It's not uncommon for couples in recovery to start over financially, sometimes with little to no savings. Handling these strains without turning to old coping mechanisms or falling into patterns of frustration and blame is essential. Establishing a clear budget that prioritizes needs, exploring financial counseling, and setting realistic financial goals as a team can reduce money-related stress. By addressing finances in an open, honest manner, both partners work together, treating finances as a shared responsibility rather than a point of contention.

Beyond practical strategies, it's important to understand the psychological toll that financial strain can take. Money issues can trigger feelings of insecurity, self-doubt, or fear about the future. Being gentle with oneself and each other during financial challenges fosters patience. Reminding each other that this phase is part of rebuilding can help alleviate fear and pressure. Viewing each step as progress, no matter how small, reinforces the idea that both partners are moving forward together, finding stability one decision at a time.

Transitions, like moving into a new home, starting a new job, or adjusting to a different daily routine, can bring stress and excitement. The shift itself often stirs uncertainty, disrupting established routines. In recovery, where structure and consistency are crucial, transitions can feel particularly destabilizing. Preparing for these changes together and talking about each person's hopes, concerns, and expectations can bring comfort. Instead of focusing on the unpredictability, couples can find strength in their ability to navigate these changes as a team, embracing each shift as a new chapter in their lives together.

With each transition, it's valuable to establish routines that support sobriety, such as regular attendance at meetings, engaging in activities that promote relaxation and joy, and staying connected with supportive communities. These routines become anchors, providing stability during times of change. Emphasizing structure over rigidity allows flexibility while maintaining the support that recovery requires. Couples can make time for rituals, like weekly date nights, to reconnect and find joy amidst new routines. Simple, shared activities remind both partners that, even in change, their relationship remains a consistent source of support.

Learning to communicate effectively during these periods of stress or transition can be transformative. When one partner is feeling overwhelmed, the other can provide a listening ear or offer support without trying to "fix" the situation. Being present for each other, without judgment or expectation, creates a safe space where both partners can openly express fears, frustrations, and hopes. By practicing empathy and understanding, couples can grow closer, knowing they have someone to lean on during life's uncertainties. This approach not only enhances individual resilience but also reinforces the relationship's foundation.

Setting realistic expectations during periods of stress and transition is equally essential. In recovery, there may be a desire to rebuild quickly or prove oneself capable after past struggles. While this motivation is positive, it can sometimes lead to disappointment if things don't progress as planned. Setting small, achievable goals and celebrating each accomplishment—no matter how minor—helps maintain motivation and prevents burnout. A steady, compassionate approach toward each step forward ensures that both partners feel encouraged rather than pressured.

Taking time to engage in self-care, both individually and as a couple, can alleviate some of the strain that comes with transitions. Practicing mindfulness, going on walks, setting aside moments for relaxation, and engaging in hobbies that bring joy are ways to reduce stress without relying on past habits. When both partners prioritize their well-being, they bring renewed energy into the relationship, creating a positive feedback loop where each person's commitment to self-care benefits the other.

Facing stress, financial strain, and life transitions isn't just about problem-solving; it's about nurturing resilience. Viewing these challenges as opportunities to grow closer rather than obstacles to be "fixed" transforms the experience. By standing together, supporting each other through the ups and downs, couples in recovery build a partnership rooted in mutual strength, understanding, and trust. Each step taken reinforces their commitment to a shared future, one defined by progress, healing, and hope.

Developing resilience as a couple in recovery is about building a partnership that withstands both life's everyday pressures and the unique challenges that come with sobriety. Resilience is the strength to keep going, together, when times are tough—a shared ability to face hardships without letting them erode the relationship or the recovery journey. For couples committed to sobriety, developing resilience isn't about avoiding difficulty; it's about learning how to stand by each other through adversity and grow stronger as a unit. Building this resilience requires intentionality, patience, and a mutual understanding that recovery isn't just a personal journey but a shared one.

One of the foundational aspects of resilience in relationships is the practice of empathy. When one partner is struggling, having the other listen without judgment or unsolicited advice creates an atmosphere of safety and respect. Often, people in recovery carry a history of trauma or difficult experiences that can resurface under stress. By creating a safe emotional space, couples cultivate trust. Instead of reacting defensively, they become each other's allies, allowing each partner to share openly, knowing they won't face blame or harsh criticism. This approach fosters resilience by building a strong emotional foundation that can withstand the strains recovery can bring.

Flexibility is another key component of resilience, as rigidity can cause frustration when things don't go as planned. Couples who practice adaptability are better equipped to handle life's surprises, whether they're related to recovery or day-to-day challenges. Flexibility doesn't mean disregarding boundaries or routines but rather finding creative ways to adjust to new situations without compromising the essentials of sobriety and mutual respect. When obstacles arise, couples who have embraced flexibility are more likely to see these moments as opportunities to grow rather than as roadblocks.

Fostering resilience also involves being proactive in addressing issues before they escalate. Small frustrations can build up over time, so regular, open communication about needs, goals, and challenges helps to prevent misunderstandings or resentments from festering. Couples can schedule periodic check-ins to discuss how each partner is feeling, any concerns, or progress in recovery. These conversations, grounded in honesty and kindness, reinforce the idea that both partners are equally invested in each other's well-being and the health of the relationship.

Developing resilience also means finding ways to navigate setbacks together without letting them derail the relationship. For couples in recovery, setbacks may occasionally happen—whether through unexpected life events, external pressures, or personal struggles. Instead of allowing setbacks to create distance, resilient couples use these moments to reinforce their commitment to each other and their recovery. When a setback does occur, it can be helpful to take a pause, assess what went wrong, and discuss ways to prevent it from happening again in a constructive, solution-focused way.

Another essential aspect of resilience is embracing shared goals and purpose. Having mutual goals can give both partners a sense of direction, and working toward something together strengthens the relationship. Whether it's saving for a shared milestone, volunteering together, or engaging in activities that promote growth, having a common purpose unites the couple beyond recovery itself. This shared sense of purpose reinforces resilience, as it gives both partners a larger context within which to view life's challenges—a reminder that their relationship is about creating a fulfilling life, not merely getting through difficulties.

Resilient couples also celebrate each other's personal achievements and milestones in recovery. Each partner brings their strengths to the relationship, and resilience is about recognizing and appreciating these qualities. Celebrating victories, no matter how small, reaffirms the couple's shared commitment to growth. By making a habit of acknowledgment and gratitude, partners create an atmosphere of positivity and support, further reinforcing resilience. This helps the relationship stay focused on progress, building a buffer against setbacks by maintaining a focus on the many steps forward taken along the way. Lastly, developing resilience as a couple means prioritizing self-care, both individually and as a unit. Recovery can be demanding, and the emotional toll of supporting each other can lead to burnout if self-care is neglected. Self-care might mean setting aside time each week to recharge individually, pursuing hobbies, or simply taking time to rest. By respecting each other's needs for self-care, partners prevent the relationship from becoming overly dependent and keep it balanced. Resilient couples understand that they must take care of themselves to show up fully for each other.

In the end, resilience isn't about having all the answers or never experiencing hardship; it's about building a relationship capable of weathering storms without losing sight of what matters. Through empathy, flexibility, shared purpose, and self-care, couples in recovery create a bond that endures beyond recovery itself—a partnership built on trust, love, and mutual commitment to growth.

Practical tools for building resilience together are essential for couples navigating recovery, as they provide structure and support to weather challenges effectively. Joint goal-setting is one of these vital tools. Setting goals together not only gives both partners a shared focus but also reinforces their commitment to mutual growth. Goals can range from short-term objectives like planning healthy routines to long-term aspirations like saving for a future milestone. By actively working on these goals, couples can strengthen their bond and create a sense of partnership that goes beyond simply staying sober. This process also allows for transparency and accountability—partners know they're working toward something meaningful as a team.

Stress-reduction techniques are equally important. Recovery, with its emotional and mental demands, can amplify stress. Finding ways to de-escalate tension individually and together is crucial. Some couples might choose to engage in mindfulness practices, such as meditation or yoga, as a shared way to ground themselves. Mindfulness helps each partner manage stress in the moment, reducing impulsive reactions and creating a calmer environment. For those less inclined toward meditation, simple breathing exercises or even shared outdoor activities like walking can be grounding. Incorporating these practices into daily routines gives both partners an outlet for stress that doesn't risk reverting to old coping mechanisms.

Establishing routines that emphasize self-care is another practical tool. Recovery is often about creating a new rhythm of life, and having a routine together can instill a sense of stability. This might involve setting regular sleep schedules, planning healthy meals, or designating time each week for connection—whether it's a quiet evening in or an outing. Routine helps to reduce the unpredictability that may trigger stress and reinforces each partner's commitment to a balanced lifestyle. It's also a reminder that sobriety isn't just a personal journey; it's a lifestyle commitment that can bring fulfillment when supported by a shared routine.

Developing effective communication strategies is another essential tool. This includes learning how to express needs, listen actively, and provide constructive feedback. Regular check-ins, where each partner takes turns speaking openly about their recovery journey, challenges, or simply their day, are a powerful way to maintain understanding. Having these honest conversations helps prevent misunderstandings from turning into conflicts, building a pattern of communication that supports long-term resilience. By practicing nonjudgmental listening, partners create a space where each feels valued and understood—a core element in maintaining both emotional and mental health in recovery. Creating a shared vision board or list of goals is an engaging way to stay focused on the future. This board could include both individual and shared aspirations—places to visit, skills to develop, or even relationship milestones to celebrate. By having these visual reminders, partners are able to stay motivated and look beyond immediate challenges. This tool also helps maintain optimism, as it keeps the couple focused on building a life they can look forward to together.

Finally, regular involvement in recovery-based groups, whether individually or together, can be a stabilizing force. These groups provide both partners with support systems outside of each other, reducing the risk of co-dependency while fostering accountability. The presence of a community also adds an extra layer of resilience, as it reminds both partners that they're not alone in their journey, allowing them to tap into collective wisdom and resources whenever needed.

In overcoming challenges together, recovery becomes more than an individual journey—it transforms into a powerful partnership rooted in resilience, understanding, and shared purpose. Through joint goals, open communication, and supportive routines, each challenge faced strengthens the bond between partners, turning obstacles into opportunities for growth. By committing to tools that foster balance and interdependence, couples build a relationship that not only withstands the tests of recovery but thrives through them. As both partners learn to support and uplift each other without falling into old patterns, they create a foundation of mutual strength, ready to embrace a future shaped by love, trust, and a shared commitment to a healthier life.

Chapter 13: Spiritual Growth and Connection

Exploring spirituality together in healing can become a deeply transformative part of recovery, offering a unique bond that enhances growth. When two people align their spiritual journey, they're not only connected by shared goals but by a mutual pursuit of meaning, purpose, and inner peace. This shared spiritual foundation doesn't have to follow traditional practices; instead, it can be uniquely crafted to resonate with both individuals, creating something personal and profound. For some couples, this might mean reconnecting with religious traditions they value, while for others, it could involve meditation, nature-based rituals, or finding meaning in everyday actions. By seeking these experiences together, partners foster trust and vulnerability, sharing parts of themselves often unseen in the routines of daily life.

Spirituality in recovery helps couples anchor themselves in values that go beyond immediate challenges, giving perspective and strength to withstand moments of doubt. In exploring spirituality, partners can encourage each other to reflect on what brings them peace and what beliefs or practices help them feel grounded. This could mean sharing books on spiritual topics, attending meetings with a spiritual focus, or simply discussing what spirituality means to each other. Conversations like these open doors to understanding one another on a deeper level, offering insights into each partner's inner world and creating a space for growth that is free of judgment.

Shared spiritual exploration often leads to increased patience, kindness, and compassion in the relationship. As partners reflect on spiritual principles—such as acceptance, gratitude, and forgiveness—they begin applying these values in their daily interactions. This approach allows for a more peaceful dynamic, reducing tension and creating a supportive environment where both people feel free to express their fears and dreams without fear of judgment. It becomes easier to give and receive forgiveness, to see each other's struggles with empathy, and to work together through difficult times with a sense of unity that extends beyond words.

Embracing spirituality as a couple often involves facing uncomfortable questions and seeking answers together. What does each partner believe about the nature of higher power or purpose? How do they make sense of life's difficulties, especially as they relate to addiction and recovery? Partners might have different answers to these questions, and that's okay; what's important is the shared willingness to engage in this exploration. Such openness deepens the relationship, as each partner learns to accept and appreciate the other's beliefs. This mutual respect allows spirituality to be a supportive foundation rather than a source of conflict, building a relationship where both partners are free to explore their faith at their own pace.

The journey toward spiritual connection also means discovering new ways to create calm and comfort together, finding activities that help both partners feel centered. This might include yoga, mindful breathing exercises, or attending spiritual gatherings together. For some couples, it's as simple as taking a walk in nature, observing the beauty around them, and talking about life's mysteries. Moments like these don't just add to spiritual growth; they create cherished memories, allowing couples to share experiences that transcend the everyday and bring them closer in ways that feel both meaningful and lasting.

In exploring spirituality together, couples often find a renewed sense of purpose in helping others, an aspect that is deeply tied to recovery. Many people in recovery find spiritual growth in service, giving back to the community, or mentoring others. Doing this as a couple strengthens the bond, showing both partners that their struggles can inspire hope and change in others' lives. It's a way to find healing beyond oneself, recognizing that recovery is a journey that connects all those impacted by addiction, creating a network of support, resilience, and shared understanding.

When spirituality becomes a shared pursuit, partners develop a strong sense of alignment that provides comfort and security. This connection allows them to draw on a common foundation of beliefs and values, especially during hard times. By building their relationship on principles that reflect a higher purpose, partners feel more prepared to tackle life's challenges with grace and gratitude. They recognize that their journey is part of something larger, a realization that brings comfort during struggles and offers a sense of peace that sustains them. As they explore spirituality, they understand that true healing is a journey of the heart, where love, compassion, and faith grow stronger each day, transforming their recovery into a shared path toward lasting peace and fulfillment.

Beliefs rooted in shared values offer couples a solid foundation in recovery, helping them face difficulties with unity and purpose. Rather than seeing challenges as obstacles to be tackled individually, these couples recognize that they have a framework guiding their decisions. With shared beliefs, both partners know they're moving in the same direction, aligned in what matters most, creating a deep sense of trust and understanding.

Shared beliefs can mean different things to different couples. For some, they're rooted in spirituality, while for others, they're grounded in mutual commitments, like compassion, kindness, or respect. Each belief, regardless of its nature, strengthens the partnership by offering a common purpose. When doubts arise, the stability of these shared values brings clarity, making it easier to move forward together.

During difficult times, shared beliefs act as an anchor. When one partner feels uncertain, the other can provide support through their mutual values, bringing them both back to a place of stability. This isn't about solving problems but about being present, offering reassurance and a reminder of the shared path they've chosen. This reliance on shared beliefs fosters a space of openness, allowing each partner to express vulnerabilities freely, knowing they'll be met with compassion and understanding.

In moments of conflict, shared beliefs become a compass for resolution. Disagreements don't center on personal victory but on finding solutions that honor their mutual values. When honesty is central, difficult truths are spoken respectfully, ensuring trust remains intact. If compassion is a priority, both partners work toward understanding rather than division. This approach transforms challenges into chances for growth, deepening their connection with each resolution.

These beliefs also encourage proactive engagement in each other's growth. Couples who value spiritual or personal development might seek activities that nurture these values, attending support groups or engaging in practices that strengthen their bond. This consistent commitment reinforces their dedication, making their relationship a mutual space for growth and resilience.

In moments of personal struggle, shared beliefs provide comfort. A partner going through a tough time knows they're supported not just by their significant other but by the values they both uphold. This shared support system is a powerful reminder of the strength they gain from their partnership, a reminder that neither has to face challenges alone. The journey through recovery becomes not just a path of individual growth but a shared journey of mutual reinforcement and deep, meaningful connection.

Spiritual connection takes many forms in recovery, each offering its own path toward growth, healing, and unity. For some, spirituality is found in structured religious practices, a source of strength that adds meaning to daily life and encourages a sense of purpose. These practices may include attending services, reading spiritual texts, or participating in faith-based support groups. In these settings, both partners find a shared space for reflection, making spirituality a central part of their lives together. Each ritual or shared experience becomes an opportunity to bond, a reminder that their relationship is rooted in values larger than themselves.

Others may find spiritual connection through mindfulness and meditation, using practices that center them in the present moment and bring clarity to their recovery journey. Mindfulness, which encourages nonjudgmental awareness of thoughts and emotions, helps couples process experiences and manage stress without becoming overwhelmed. When practiced together, meditation fosters a sense of peace and trust, encouraging both partners to listen deeply, not just to each other but to their own inner needs. Setting aside a few minutes each day for shared meditation or guided visualization strengthens the connection between partners while promoting individual calmness and self-awareness.

Some couples approach spirituality through nature, finding connection and healing in outdoor experiences. Nature walks, hikes, or even simple moments spent observing the natural world remind them of their place in the larger tapestry of life. This approach allows them to disconnect from the distractions of daily life and reconnect with themselves and each other on a fundamental level. Nature can offer a perspective that quiets anxieties and brings a sense of harmony, making it easier to see beyond immediate struggles and appreciate the shared beauty of their journey. Time spent outdoors becomes a grounding ritual that reinforces their bond.

Artistic expression provides another path for spiritual connection, especially for couples who resonate with creativity. Through activities like painting, writing, or music, partners explore inner landscapes, expressing feelings that may be challenging to put into words. Creating art together or supporting each other's creative endeavors invites a vulnerability that strengthens trust, opening a space where both feel safe to share and understand each other's emotional experiences. These moments of shared creativity foster a deep, unspoken connection, a sense that they are witnessing each other's growth and transformation in profound, meaningful ways.

Many find spiritual connection through acts of service, recognizing that giving back can be a form of healing. Volunteering together or supporting each other's service efforts brings fulfillment and a shared sense of purpose. Acts of kindness, whether within their recovery communities or beyond, build compassion and reinforce a mindset of gratitude. Each act, no matter how small, becomes a reminder that their journey extends beyond themselves, that the love and support they share can have a ripple effect on those around them. This commitment to helping others brings a powerful sense of spiritual fulfillment, affirming the values they're working to live by in recovery.

For others, spiritual connection may mean simply sharing a space of gratitude. Expressing appreciation regularly, whether verbally or in a shared gratitude journal, encourages a positive outlook that supports both partners. This daily practice brings light to even the most challenging moments, fostering resilience and nurturing a shared sense of joy. Over time, gratitude becomes an anchor, helping both partners maintain perspective and focus on the positives in their journey together.

Different paths to spiritual connection allow couples to explore what feels most authentic and meaningful to them. There is no single approach, and their spiritual practices may evolve as they grow. As they try different paths, they gain a deeper understanding of each other's needs and values, discovering new ways to connect that are deeply personal. Together, they create a unique spiritual language, a bond that sustains them in moments of difficulty and celebration alike. This shared spiritual foundation becomes a source of strength, bringing them closer and enhancing their journey in recovery.

Incorporating practical spiritual tools can deepen a couple's connection, adding layers of shared meaning and support in their recovery journey. Guided meditations, gratitude lists, and spiritual journaling are ways to bring spirituality into daily life, offering structured methods that both partners can rely on to stay centered, connected, and resilient.

One tool is guided meditation, which can provide focus and intention to each day. By practicing this together, couples build a routine that enhances presence and mindfulness, allowing them to handle challenges with greater calm. They might start each morning or end each evening with a short, five- or ten-minute guided meditation that centers around themes like gratitude, love, or self-compassion. Choosing a guided meditation that resonates with both partners, whether found on an app or created by themselves, strengthens their shared commitment to being present. Guided meditation can also be a way to reflect on specific recovery goals, allowing both to visualize a path forward and maintain perspective during moments of stress.

Shared gratitude lists add another level of spiritual connection by helping couples focus on the positives and practice appreciation. Each day, they might write down a few things they are grateful for, big or small, that uplift or support them. This could include moments in their relationship, support from others, or progress made in recovery. Over time, the habit of expressing gratitude together shifts focus away from challenges or obstacles and toward the blessings they share, creating a positive feedback loop that reinforces their bond. A shared journal for gratitude lists can also be a treasured keepsake, something to look back on that reminds them of how far they've come and the joy they've found together.

Incorporating spirituality into daily routines also works well through joint reading practices, particularly if both partners find inspiration in certain texts, whether spiritual books, recovery literature, or self-help guides. Setting aside a few minutes each day to read and discuss a passage or a chapter creates intentional time for reflection. These readings can spark meaningful conversations and bring new perspectives to shared goals or values. Books or devotionals that speak to both partners allow them to build a shared understanding, promoting a deeper sense of unity and direction. Keeping a book on hand that they turn to together can become a cherished part of their daily or weekly routine, helping them stay grounded.

Another powerful tool is creating personal affirmations or mantras, words that reinforce shared intentions. By developing a set of affirmations together, couples can focus on their mutual goals, whether related to recovery, relationship growth, or individual well-being. These affirmations can be posted in a shared space like the bathroom mirror or kept in a journal, a tangible reminder of their goals. Reciting or silently reflecting on these affirmations during the day can be a grounding exercise that keeps both partners aligned. Simple statements like "We support each other's growth," or "Our relationship is a safe space for healing" reinforce their shared values, bringing focus and intention into each day.

Spiritual journaling provides an opportunity for reflection and connection, giving both partners a way to process thoughts, feelings, and challenges individually and together. Each person can have their own journal for self-reflection and occasionally share passages that resonate with their journey. This sharing can deepen understanding, foster empathy, and create space for vulnerability. Journaling as a couple, whether in a shared book or individually, encourages openness and honesty while providing an outlet for emotions that might be difficult to express in conversation alone. Setting aside time weekly or monthly to read entries together creates a sense of ritual that strengthens their connection and brings clarity to their journey as a couple.

Acts of service or volunteer work can also be spiritual tools that bring couples closer while benefiting others. Choosing to volunteer together, whether through local recovery programs, community service, or charity work, offers a shared purpose. Giving back, especially when motivated by gratitude and empathy, strengthens the relationship by adding layers of compassion and shared growth. Whether it's helping to organize events, mentoring others in recovery, or assisting community initiatives, acts of service help couples connect with each other in a meaningful way. These experiences also reinforce the idea that their journey is not only about individual growth but about extending support and kindness to those around them.

Participating in support groups or recovery-related spiritual gatherings can also create community and broaden spiritual perspectives. Attending meetings or events together, whether in person or virtually, fosters a sense of shared experience and connects couples with others on similar journeys. Being part of a community committed to recovery can be immensely strengthening, providing a shared sense of accountability and belonging. It's also an opportunity for couples to see recovery and spirituality through the eyes of others, expanding their perspectives and deepening their own connection.

Finally, setting shared spiritual goals can be a grounding, growth-centered practice. Whether it's aiming to read a set number of spiritual or recovery-focused books together, attending workshops, or creating personal growth plans, these goals add structure to the relationship's spiritual journey. Achieving these milestones together not only adds fulfillment but serves as a reminder of their dedication to growing alongside each other. These goals can be reevaluated periodically, allowing for adjustments as each partner's needs or perspectives evolve.

Each of these tools supports a different aspect of spiritual growth, bringing flexibility to the ways couples can foster connection. In using them, couples develop habits and practices that enhance resilience, provide grounding, and keep their relationship rooted in shared values. As these tools become part of daily life, they enrich the journey, creating a relationship that feels balanced, open, and spiritually alive.

The exploration of spiritual growth and connection in recovery reveals how couples can enhance their bond while navigating the challenges of sobriety. Engaging in practices like guided meditations, shared gratitude lists, and spiritual journaling allows partners to deepen their understanding of one another and support each other's healing processes. As they embrace shared beliefs and values, couples create a solid foundation that helps them weather life's storms and celebrate each other's successes. These tools encourage ongoing communication and reflection, fostering resilience and empathy as they evolve both individually and as a couple. By prioritizing spiritual growth, partners can cultivate a lasting relationship rooted in love, compassion, and shared purpose, illuminating their path through recovery and enriching their shared experiences along the way.

Chapter 14: Maintaining Individuality in Relationships

Balancing personal growth with relationship needs is essential for couples navigating recovery together. Each partner must embark on their individual journey of self-discovery and healing while simultaneously nurturing the connection they share. Personal growth involves exploring one's values, passions, and goals, allowing for a deeper understanding of oneself. This self-awareness can significantly enhance the relationship, as individuals bring a more authentic version of themselves into the partnership. However, it's crucial that personal development does not overshadow the relational dynamics that also require attention and care.

In recovery, personal growth often comes from engaging in various activities that foster individual strengths. This could involve pursuing new hobbies, participating in support groups, or seeking therapy to address past trauma. Each person's journey is unique, and it's vital for partners to respect and support each other's pursuits. Encouraging one another to engage in personal interests not only promotes a healthy sense of independence but also enriches the relationship by introducing new experiences and perspectives.

It is equally important to ensure that personal growth does not become a source of disconnection between partners. Regular communication is key to maintaining a balance. Open discussions about personal goals, challenges, and successes can foster a sense of shared experience, even when pursuing individual paths. Couples should set aside time to check in with each other, discussing their growth while also addressing any feelings of neglect or imbalance that may arise. This mutual understanding helps create a safe space where both partners feel heard and valued.

Creating shared goals can also be an effective strategy for balancing personal growth with relationship needs. These goals can range from planning activities that both partners enjoy to setting recovery milestones that they can celebrate together. For instance, attending a workshop or retreat focused on personal development as a couple can enhance their bond while allowing each partner to pursue their individual growth. These shared experiences contribute to a stronger foundation, making it easier to navigate any challenges that may arise in the relationship.

It is essential to acknowledge that personal growth can sometimes lead to significant changes in the dynamics of a relationship. As individuals grow and evolve, their needs and expectations may shift. This is where flexibility becomes vital. Both partners should remain open to redefining their roles and responsibilities within the relationship. Compromise is a necessary component, allowing each person to feel fulfilled in their personal journey while still prioritizing the needs of the partnership.

Support systems outside the relationship can also play a crucial role in balancing personal growth with relationship needs. Engaging with friends, family, or support groups provides individuals with additional outlets for expressing their thoughts and feelings. This external support can alleviate pressure on the romantic relationship, as partners can draw strength from a wider community. It also prevents one partner from feeling solely responsible for the other's emotional well-being.

Another aspect to consider is the importance of self-care. Both partners should prioritize their well-being, as it directly impacts the relationship. When individuals practice self-care, they are better equipped to contribute positively to their partnership. This includes physical, emotional, and mental well-being. Regularly engaging in activities that replenish their energy and promote happiness helps each partner bring their best self to the relationship.

Balancing personal growth with relationship needs does not mean neglecting each partner's individual journey. Instead, it is about recognizing the interplay between self-improvement and the health of the relationship. Both aspects can coexist and thrive when approached with intention and care. By maintaining open lines of communication, establishing shared goals, and prioritizing self-care, couples can create a harmonious environment that supports both personal development and relational fulfillment.

In the realm of recovery, this balance becomes even more significant. Each partner's progress can inspire the other, fostering a cycle of growth that benefits the entire relationship. Recognizing the unique contributions each person brings to the partnership allows couples to appreciate their shared journey while celebrating their individual victories. Embracing this holistic approach to growth ensures that both partners remain invested in the relationship while pursuing their personal paths. In this way, couples can build a strong foundation that supports both individual aspirations and the health of their partnership, creating a fulfilling and resilient bond that withstands the challenges of recovery.

Encouraging independence and interests within a relationship is crucial, especially in recovery. As individuals heal from past traumas and addictive behaviors, fostering a sense of autonomy allows partners to grow both as individuals and as a couple. Independence is not about creating distance; rather, it is about building a foundation of trust and self-confidence that can enhance the relationship. Each partner's pursuit of their own interests can lead to a more balanced and fulfilling partnership, where both individuals feel valued and respected.

The journey of recovery often emphasizes the importance of personal identity. Many individuals in recovery may have lost sight of who they are outside of their past behaviors and struggles. Encouraging each partner to explore their own interests can facilitate this rediscovery process. Whether it's pursuing a new hobby, engaging in sports, or taking up creative arts, each individual should feel empowered to embrace what makes them unique. Allowing each other the freedom to explore these interests strengthens their emotional connection and provides a supportive environment for growth.

Recognizing that pursuing personal interests does not equate to abandoning the relationship is vital. Engaging in separate activities can enrich the partnership by bringing fresh experiences and insights into the relationship. When each partner is actively involved in their passions, they have more to share and discuss with one another. This dynamic fosters a deeper understanding of each other's lives. Encouraging independence can be as simple as setting aside time for personal activities without guilt or resentment, allowing each partner to recharge and return to the relationship with renewed energy.

Open communication plays a significant role in fostering independence within the relationship. Discussing individual interests and goals can help create a sense of support. Each partner should express their needs and desires regarding personal time and activities. This dialogue ensures that both partners feel heard and respected in their pursuits. If one partner feels stifled or overly dependent on the other for emotional support, it can lead to resentment or frustration. By discussing these feelings openly, couples can work toward finding a healthy balance that respects each individual's need for independence while still prioritizing their connection.

Setting boundaries is essential when encouraging independence. Each partner should establish personal limits that allow them to engage in their interests while still being present for one another. If one partner enjoys spending time with friends, it's crucial to communicate this desire openly while ensuring that quality time together remains a priority. Establishing these boundaries creates a safe space where both partners can thrive individually without compromising the relationship.

Supporting each other in pursuing educational or professional goals is another way to encourage independence. As individuals grow, they may feel inspired to continue their education or develop new career paths. When partners uplift and encourage each other's ambitions, it fosters a sense of teamwork and shared success. Celebrating milestones in personal growth, such as completing a course or achieving a career goal, strengthens the emotional bond and creates a shared sense of accomplishment within the relationship.

Creating a supportive environment for independence also involves recognizing and respecting each partner's emotional needs. It's important to acknowledge that while independence is crucial, there will be times when one partner may need extra support due to challenges in recovery. During these moments, being responsive to each other's needs can help maintain a healthy balance. Practicing empathy and understanding allows partners to navigate the complexities of recovery together while still honoring their independence.

Incorporating joint activities that promote individual interests can be beneficial. Couples can create opportunities to engage in activities together that allow for personal expression. If one partner enjoys painting and the other loves music, they can spend an afternoon creating art while listening to their favorite tunes. This approach nurtures individuality and fosters connection and collaboration, reinforcing the idea that both partners can flourish together while pursuing their passions.

Encouraging independence also means understanding that it's okay to have differing interests. Partners should embrace their unique preferences and be open to exploring each other's hobbies. This exploration can lead to new experiences that both individuals may not have considered before. For example, one partner might discover a love for hiking through their partner's passion for outdoor adventures, fostering a shared interest that enriches the relationship while allowing for personal enjoyment.

Celebrating each other's successes and milestones in pursuing independence reinforces the idea that individual growth is a shared journey. Recognizing achievements, no matter how small, contributes to a positive atmosphere within the relationship. This acknowledgment can serve as motivation for both partners to continue striving for personal goals while remaining supportive of one another.

Fostering independence in a relationship requires continuous reflection and adjustment. As individuals grow and evolve, their needs and desires may change. Partners should regularly check in with each other to ensure that their approach to independence remains healthy and balanced. This ongoing dialogue helps prevent misunderstandings and promotes a sense of security within the relationship.

Encouraging independence and interests is about creating a partnership where both individuals feel empowered to grow while remaining connected. Recovery is a journey that requires personal exploration, and couples who support each other's individuality can cultivate a strong foundation for lasting love and fulfillment. By embracing personal interests, maintaining open communication, setting boundaries, and celebrating each other's successes, couples can thrive together in their recovery journey, nurturing a relationship that honors both independence and intimacy.

Avoiding losing oneself in a relationship is essential for maintaining a healthy dynamic, particularly in recovery. It's easy to become so entwined in a partner's life that individual identities blur, leading to co-dependency and feelings of emptiness. Recovery often demands introspection and self-discovery, and it's crucial that both partners prioritize their sense of self while nurturing their connection. Balancing togetherness and individuality is the key to thriving in a relationship.

Personal identity can sometimes feel fragile, especially after significant life changes such as entering recovery. Individuals may have spent years defining themselves through their struggles, and emerging from those experiences can lead to uncertainty about who they are outside of the addiction. It's vital to remember that each partner in a relationship brings unique qualities, strengths, and interests. Engaging in activities and interests that foster self-awareness can help individuals rediscover their identities. Partners should encourage one another to pursue passions, hobbies, and friendships outside the relationship, creating a diverse support network that enriches their lives.

Setting boundaries is fundamental to maintaining individuality. Boundaries provide a framework for what each partner needs from the relationship and allow for personal space and growth. This doesn't mean building walls; rather, it involves openly communicating needs and desires. If one partner enjoys spending time with friends or engaging in solo activities, establishing boundaries around these preferences can help create a more balanced relationship. Recognizing that it's okay to have separate lives fosters a sense of security and trust between partners.

Time management plays a significant role in avoiding the loss of self. Couples should actively allocate time for personal activities and interests. Creating a schedule that includes both individual and shared activities ensures that each partner has the opportunity to engage in their pursuits without feeling guilty. This structured approach can help prevent feelings of resentment or obligation that may arise when one partner feels their needs are consistently sidelined. Balancing individual time and couple time can lead to a more satisfying and enriching relationship.

Self-care is a crucial aspect of avoiding the loss of self. Recovery can be demanding, both emotionally and physically. Each partner must prioritize their well-being through self-care practices that nurture their body, mind, and spirit. Engaging in self-care routines—whether it's exercise, meditation, reading, or spending time in nature—allows individuals to recharge and reconnect with themselves. When partners take care of their own needs, they are better equipped to support each other, ultimately benefiting the relationship.

Developing self-awareness is another vital aspect of maintaining individuality. Each partner should reflect on their thoughts, feelings, and behaviors, understanding how they impact the relationship. Self-awareness encourages honest communication and fosters an environment where both partners feel safe expressing their needs. Journaling can be an effective tool for self-reflection, allowing individuals to process their experiences and emotions. By gaining insight into their thoughts and feelings, partners can better navigate challenges together without losing sight of their individuality.

Encouraging open dialogue about personal needs and desires promotes a culture of respect and understanding. Partners should feel comfortable discussing their aspirations, concerns, and boundaries without fear of judgment. This ongoing communication ensures that both partners remain engaged in each other's lives while preserving their unique identities. Regular check-ins can help partners assess whether they feel their individual needs are being met and make adjustments if necessary.

Creating a balance between intimacy and independence involves recognizing that both are essential for a healthy relationship. Couples should celebrate their closeness while also honoring their autonomy. This balance can be achieved by establishing rituals that promote connection—such as regular date nights—while also maintaining individual pursuits. Engaging in shared activities that reflect both partners' interests allows for mutual growth while reinforcing their bond.

Recognizing when one partner feels overwhelmed or lost in the relationship is vital. Signs may include withdrawal from personal interests, a decline in emotional well-being, or a sense of obligation rather than enjoyment in the partnership. Partners should be attuned to these changes and willing to address them openly. Encouraging conversations about feelings can help identify areas where one partner may feel stifled or neglected, allowing for proactive solutions that prioritize individuality.

It's important to celebrate each other's successes outside the relationship. Acknowledging personal achievements, whether big or small, fosters an environment of support and encouragement. Celebrating milestones in individual pursuits reinforces the idea that both partners are equally valued, regardless of their role within the relationship. This celebration of individuality enhances the emotional connection between partners, creating a deeper appreciation for one another.

Maintaining friendships outside the relationship is crucial for avoiding co-dependency. Having a support network provides each partner with additional outlets for emotional expression and social interaction. Friends can offer perspectives and encouragement that may not always come from within the relationship. Encouraging each other to spend time with friends helps prevent feelings of isolation and promotes a sense of community. Each partner should have the freedom to nurture outside relationships without guilt or fear.

Cultivating shared experiences is also essential for preventing the loss of self. Engaging in activities that both partners enjoy allows them to create memories while still honoring their individuality. Shared experiences should not overshadow personal pursuits; rather, they should complement them. Finding common interests can strengthen the bond between partners while also providing opportunities for personal growth.

As relationships evolve, the risk of losing oneself can increase, especially during stressful times. Recovery may bring challenges that test the strength of the partnership, leading individuals to prioritize the relationship at the expense of their own identity. It's crucial to remain vigilant and proactive in nurturing individuality. By fostering an environment where both partners feel empowered to pursue their interests and growth, couples can navigate the complexities of their journey together without losing sight of who they are as individuals.

Ultimately, maintaining a strong sense of self within a relationship is vital for personal growth and mutual support. Partners should actively encourage each other to pursue their passions, set boundaries, and engage in open communication about their needs. By doing so, they create a relationship that honors both their individuality and their connection, allowing them to thrive together in recovery. Embracing personal growth alongside shared experiences fosters a partnership built on mutual respect, understanding, and love.

Fostering individuality within a relationship is essential for both personal growth and partnership strength. By prioritizing independent interests and engaging in activities that nurture each partner's unique identity, couples can create a balanced dynamic that supports mutual respect and connection. Implementing practical tools, such as individual project lists, solo retreats, and mindfulness practices, encourages each partner to flourish while maintaining a strong bond. Celebrating personal achievements, nurturing friendships, and creating shared goals reinforce the idea that each individual's journey enriches the partnership. As couples embrace the importance of individuality, they cultivate a healthier, more resilient relationship that honors both personal and shared aspirations, ultimately leading to a deeper and more fulfilling connection.

Chapter 15: Growing Old in Sobriety Together

Long-term relationships undergo significant transformation, especially in the context of recovery. As individuals navigate their sobriety journey, they not only confront personal challenges but also encounter changes that impact their partnerships. The evolution of a relationship in recovery can be a beautiful and enriching experience, deepening bonds as partners learn to support each other's growth while facing the realities of life without substances. In early recovery, couples often experience a heightened sense of vulnerability and emotional intensity. This period, while challenging, serves as a crucial time for developing communication skills, trust, and intimacy. As both partners begin to embrace sobriety, they may discover new aspects of themselves and their relationship dynamics, forcing them to confront old patterns and assumptions that no longer serve them.

As time passes, couples in long-term recovery must navigate the complexities of life together, including career changes, family dynamics, and health issues. These changes can strengthen the partnership or create tension, depending on how the couple approaches them. The ability to communicate openly and honestly becomes vital during this stage, as partners learn to express their needs and expectations while also remaining attuned to one another's emotions. The growth of emotional intelligence fosters a deeper connection, allowing couples to approach challenges as a united front. This shared journey often leads to a new level of understanding and empathy, creating a foundation for a healthy, supportive relationship.

A key element in the evolution of long-term relationships in recovery is the recognition of interdependence. Unlike co-dependence, which can foster unhealthy dynamics, interdependence encourages partners to rely on one another for support while still maintaining their individuality. Each partner learns to recognize their strengths and weaknesses and how they can complement one another. This balance allows for a healthier relationship dynamic where both individuals feel valued and appreciated. As partners grow in their sobriety, they also develop shared values, goals, and dreams that reflect their commitment to one another and their recovery journey.

Navigating life's ups and downs together can also bring about shared experiences that create lasting memories. Couples in recovery often find solace in engaging in new activities, exploring interests, and traveling together. These experiences provide opportunities to strengthen their bond and foster deeper emotional intimacy. The challenges they face together, whether they be overcoming personal setbacks or celebrating milestones in recovery, become part of their shared narrative, enriching the story of their relationship. As they face obstacles, couples learn the importance of teamwork, resilience, and adaptability, skills that are crucial for long-term success in both sobriety and their partnership.

Moreover, long-term sobriety often encourages couples to engage in healthier communication patterns. As they practice active listening and express their feelings more openly, partners can work through conflicts in a constructive manner. This shift leads to a deeper understanding of each other's needs and desires, fostering an environment where both individuals feel heard and respected. Emotional vulnerability becomes a source of strength, allowing partners to share their fears and aspirations without fear of judgment. As trust deepens, so does the commitment to nurturing the relationship, leading to a more profound emotional connection.

Additionally, long-term relationships in recovery may face the challenge of external influences, such as societal pressures or the presence of old acquaintances who may not understand or respect their sobriety. Couples must develop strategies to protect their relationship from these potential pitfalls, reinforcing their commitment to one another and their shared goals. This may involve setting clear boundaries with friends or family members who do not support their recovery, thereby creating a safe space for their relationship to thrive. Building a strong support network can also be invaluable, as surrounding themselves with like-minded individuals who understand the challenges of recovery can foster a sense of community and belonging.

Ultimately, the evolution of long-term relationships in sobriety is a testament to the power of love, commitment, and shared growth. As couples navigate the complexities of life together, they learn the importance of adaptability, communication, and mutual respect. Embracing change and facing challenges together enables partners to cultivate a strong foundation built on trust and understanding. The journey of recovery not only transforms individuals but also shapes the very essence of their relationships. By celebrating their successes and supporting one another through difficulties, couples can create a lasting bond that stands the test of time, growing stronger as they age together in sobriety.

Facing new challenges as life changes is an inherent aspect of long-term relationships in recovery. The dynamic nature of life means that couples will inevitably encounter a range of transitions that test their commitment and resilience. As partners grow older, they will likely face new obstacles, such as career shifts, health issues, the aging process, and evolving family dynamics. Each of these changes can impact the relationship, requiring couples to adapt and grow together in the face of adversity.

Career changes can be particularly challenging, as they often come with heightened stress, shifts in financial stability, and a need to recalibrate roles within the partnership. When one partner experiences a job loss or a transition to a new career, it can create a sense of insecurity or uncertainty. Navigating this challenge requires open communication and a willingness to support one another through the emotional and practical implications of these changes. Partners must work together to set new financial goals and establish plans that reflect their evolving circumstances. This may involve reassessing household responsibilities, prioritizing expenses, or seeking new opportunities for professional development. By approaching these challenges collaboratively, couples can strengthen their bond and foster a sense of unity amid uncertainty. Health issues, whether physical or mental, can also present significant challenges for couples in long-term recovery. As individuals age, they may encounter chronic health conditions or experience changes in their physical capabilities. Additionally, the emotional toll of dealing with health-related challenges can create stress within the relationship. In these situations, partners must cultivate patience and empathy as they navigate the complexities of supporting one another. Developing a shared understanding of how health issues impact both individuals is crucial for maintaining a balanced relationship. Encouraging open dialogue about concerns, fears, and treatment options allows couples to navigate the realities of health challenges together.

Family dynamics often shift as partners grow older, whether through changes in the roles of children, aging parents, or evolving family relationships. Couples may find themselves taking on new responsibilities, such as caring for aging parents or supporting their children as they navigate their own challenges. These shifts can lead to feelings of overwhelm or resentment if partners do not communicate openly about their feelings and expectations. Prioritizing discussions about family roles and responsibilities can help alleviate misunderstandings and foster a supportive environment. By sharing the load and recognizing each other's contributions, couples can navigate these challenges together, reinforcing their commitment to one another and their shared values.

New challenges in long-term relationships can also stem from external influences. Friends or family members may not fully understand the intricacies of a couple's recovery journey, leading to potential misunderstandings or conflicts. Couples must establish clear boundaries with those who may inadvertently jeopardize their sobriety or well-being. This may involve explaining the importance of maintaining a sober lifestyle and the need for mutual support within their relationship. By asserting their boundaries and standing firm in their commitment to sobriety, couples can navigate external pressures and foster a stronger bond based on mutual respect.

Transitioning into new phases of life, such as retirement, can also present both challenges and opportunities. As individuals shift from a structured work environment to a more flexible schedule, they may experience feelings of loss or uncertainty about their identity. This transition can impact the couple dynamic as partners must renegotiate their roles and find new ways to connect. Embracing this change requires open dialogue about aspirations, goals, and the desire for continued growth as individuals and as a couple. Engaging in new activities, pursuing shared interests, and exploring hobbies together can help foster a sense of connection and purpose during this time of transition.

Amid these challenges, couples in long-term recovery must remain vigilant in maintaining their own well-being while supporting one another. Individual self-care practices play a crucial role in navigating life changes effectively. Prioritizing time for personal growth, engaging in hobbies, and seeking support through therapy or support groups can equip individuals with the tools necessary to cope with stressors and maintain their sobriety. When partners focus on their personal well-being, they contribute positively to the overall health of the relationship.

Establishing shared goals is another vital aspect of facing new challenges together. As life changes, couples can work collaboratively to set new objectives that reflect their evolving priorities. These goals can encompass various aspects of life, such as financial planning, health and wellness initiatives, travel aspirations, or personal growth endeavors. By involving each partner in the goal-setting process, couples create a sense of shared purpose and commitment to one another. This collaborative approach fosters unity and strengthens the relationship as partners support each other in achieving their aspirations.

As couples confront the inevitability of life changes, their ability to adapt and grow together becomes paramount. Navigating challenges requires ongoing communication, vulnerability, and a willingness to embrace the unknown. Couples must remember that they are not alone in their journey and that seeking external support, whether through counseling, support groups, or trusted friends, can provide valuable guidance and perspective.

The evolution of a relationship in recovery is a continuous journey marked by ups and downs, victories and setbacks. Each new challenge faced together can serve as an opportunity for growth and transformation, reinforcing the bonds of love and support that define the partnership. By fostering open communication, establishing boundaries, and remaining committed to individual and shared growth, couples can successfully navigate the complexities of life changes, emerging stronger and more connected than ever. Ultimately, the resilience cultivated in the face of challenges not only solidifies the partnership but also enhances the overall quality of life for both individuals.

Embracing the journey of sober life together becomes a pivotal aspect of a long-term relationship rooted in recovery. The decision to walk this path not only reflects a commitment to sobriety but also signifies a shared dedication to building a life filled with purpose, joy, and connection. As partners navigate the challenges and triumphs of sobriety, they create a unique bond that is strengthened through shared experiences, mutual support, and a collective vision for the future.

Walking the journey of sobriety is not a solitary endeavor. It involves facing various obstacles, from cravings and triggers to societal pressures and personal fears. Each partner's commitment to maintaining their sobriety serves as a foundation upon which the relationship can thrive. This shared commitment fosters an environment of trust and understanding, where both individuals can openly discuss their struggles and celebrate their victories without judgment. Supporting one another through difficult moments not only reinforces their bond but also serves as a reminder of the strength that comes from partnership.

The journey of sober life together also provides opportunities for personal growth and self-discovery. Each partner may find themselves learning new coping strategies, exploring healthier habits, and developing deeper emotional resilience. Engaging in individual recovery activities, such as therapy, support groups, or mindfulness practices, can enhance personal growth while simultaneously benefiting the relationship. Couples can share insights gained through these activities, fostering deeper conversations that strengthen their emotional connection.

Celebrating milestones in sobriety becomes an essential part of embracing the journey together. Acknowledging achievements, whether big or small, fosters a sense of accomplishment and reinforces the positive changes being made. Couples can create traditions around celebrating these milestones, such as having a special dinner, going on a trip, or simply taking time to reflect on their progress together. These celebrations not only honor the hard work put into sobriety but also remind both partners of the positive life they are building together.

Exploring new activities and interests as a couple can also enhance the journey of sobriety. Trying new hobbies, participating in community events, or engaging in fitness activities together creates shared experiences that deepen the relationship. These moments of joy and connection help reinforce the idea that life in sobriety can be fulfilling and exciting. They allow couples to create new memories and redefine their relationship beyond addiction.

Communication plays a vital role in embracing this journey. Open discussions about feelings, fears, and aspirations create a safe space for partners to express themselves. As they navigate the complexities of sober life, partners should encourage honesty and vulnerability, allowing each individual to feel heard and understood. This ongoing dialogue fosters empathy and strengthens the emotional intimacy within the relationship, which is essential for sustaining a healthy partnership in recovery.

Embracing the journey of sober life together also involves a commitment to self-care. Each partner must prioritize their well-being to contribute positively to the relationship. Engaging in self-care practices—whether it's exercise, meditation, spending time with supportive friends, or pursuing personal interests—allows individuals to recharge and maintain their mental health. A balanced approach to self-care ensures that both partners can show up fully for each other, fostering a healthier dynamic within the relationship.

As couples navigate the ups and downs of sobriety, it is essential to remain adaptable. Life in recovery can be unpredictable, with unexpected challenges arising at any moment. Being flexible and willing to adjust to changing circumstances fosters resilience and strengthens the partnership. Couples can work together to develop strategies for handling stressors, ensuring that they face challenges as a united front.

The journey of sober life together also includes addressing past traumas and unresolved issues that may impact the relationship. Couples should prioritize working through these challenges, whether through therapy or open conversations. Acknowledging and addressing past wounds allows for healing and growth, creating a healthier foundation for the future. This process reinforces the idea that the journey of sobriety is not just about avoiding substances but also about healing emotional scars and building a life filled with love and support.

In addition to addressing past issues, couples can also focus on building new traditions that honor their sober lifestyle. Establishing rituals—whether it's weekly date nights, monthly outings, or annual trips—provides opportunities for connection and joy. These shared experiences create lasting memories and reinforce the idea that sobriety does not mean sacrificing fun or excitement; rather, it opens the door to new adventures.

Recognizing the importance of gratitude is another crucial aspect of embracing the journey together. Taking time to reflect on the positive aspects of their lives and the progress made in sobriety fosters a mindset of appreciation. Couples can incorporate gratitude practices into their routine, such as sharing what they are thankful for during dinner or keeping a joint gratitude journal. This practice reinforces the positive aspects of their lives and encourages a focus on the present moment.

Embracing the journey of sober life together also means advocating for each other's recovery. Each partner should support the other in seeking additional resources, whether it's attending support groups, engaging in therapy, or exploring holistic practices. Being an advocate for each other's recovery fosters a sense of partnership and ensures that both individuals feel supported in their journeys.

Lastly, couples should remember that the journey of sobriety is ongoing. It requires constant reflection, adaptation, and growth. By committing to this shared journey, couples build a foundation of trust and resilience that can withstand life's challenges. Embracing the journey together means continually seeking ways to strengthen their bond, celebrate their successes, and navigate obstacles as a team. It is this dedication to each other and the journey that ultimately leads to a fulfilling and meaningful life in sobriety. As partners navigate the complexities of life, their commitment to each other becomes a source of strength and inspiration, propelling them forward on the path of recovery together.

Practical tools for couples in recovery provide essential resources to navigate their shared journey of sobriety while enhancing their emotional connection. Reflection prompts and future planning activities serve as effective methods for couples to deepen their understanding of one another, address individual needs, and align their goals for the future. These tools create opportunities for meaningful conversations, fostering an environment where both partners feel heard, supported, and motivated.

Reflection prompts can be a powerful way to facilitate deep conversations about the recovery experience. They encourage partners to explore their thoughts, feelings, and behaviors, which can lead to greater insights into themselves and each other. Simple prompts, such as "What have been the most significant challenges in our recovery journey together?" or "How has our relationship changed since we began this journey?" allow couples to reflect on their experiences and articulate their feelings. Discussing these prompts can help partners recognize patterns in their relationship, identify areas for growth, and appreciate their progress.

Additionally, couples can use reflection prompts to explore their individual journeys. Questions like "What personal challenges have you faced in recovery?" or "What are some accomplishments you're proud of?" encourage open dialogue and validation. This practice fosters empathy and understanding as partners share their experiences, allowing them to connect on a deeper level. Understanding each other's struggles and triumphs strengthens the emotional bond, creating a supportive atmosphere where both partners feel valued.

Future planning activities play a crucial role in shaping a shared vision for the relationship. These activities can range from setting short-term goals to discussing long-term aspirations. Couples can start by discussing what they envision for their lives in recovery. Questions like

"What are our individual goals for the next year?" or "How do we see ourselves growing together in the future?" help partners clarify their desires and align their aspirations. This planning process creates a sense of shared purpose, reinforcing their commitment to each other and their recovery.

Creating a vision board is a fun and engaging activity that allows couples to visualize their goals and dreams. Each partner can gather images, quotes, or words that represent their aspirations and create a collage. Displaying the vision board in a prominent place serves as a daily reminder of their shared goals and encourages ongoing discussions about progress. This visual representation of their future fosters motivation and inspiration, reminding couples of their commitment to growth and connection.

Another practical tool for future planning is developing a shared calendar that includes important dates, goals, and milestones. Couples can mark anniversaries, sobriety milestones, and planned activities, ensuring they prioritize quality time together. This calendar serves as a guide for maintaining a balanced relationship while pursuing individual interests. It also provides opportunities for celebration, encouraging couples to acknowledge and honor their accomplishments along the way.

To further enhance future planning, couples can establish regular check-in sessions dedicated to discussing their goals and progress. Setting aside time each week or month to review their objectives fosters accountability and encourages open communication. During these check-ins, partners can discuss what has been working, what challenges they are facing, and how they can support each other moving forward. This structured approach helps couples stay focused on their goals and reinforces their commitment to growth.

Exploring new activities together also contributes to future planning. Couples can identify shared interests or hobbies they wish to pursue as a way to enhance their relationship. Trying out new experiences, whether it's taking a cooking class, going on hikes, or attending community events, provides opportunities for bonding and fun. Engaging in these activities together helps couples create new memories and strengthens their connection in a positive, fulfilling way. In addition to discussing shared goals, partners should also make space for individual aspirations. Encouraging each other to pursue personal interests and hobbies fosters independence and growth within the relationship. Couples can share their individual goals and discuss how they can support each other in achieving them. This balance between shared and individual aspirations creates a healthier dynamic, ensuring both partners feel fulfilled while contributing to the relationship.

It's essential for couples to periodically revisit and revise their goals and plans. Life in recovery is dynamic, and circumstances can change. Regularly assessing their aspirations allows couples to remain flexible and adapt to new challenges or opportunities. This ongoing dialogue about goals reinforces the idea that they are partners in both life and recovery, supporting each other through various phases of their journey.

Another effective practical tool for couples is the use of gratitude exercises to reinforce positivity and connection. Taking time to reflect on what they appreciate about each other can enhance emotional intimacy. Couples can create a gratitude jar where they regularly add notes of appreciation for one another. On special occasions, they can read these notes together, celebrating the love and support they share. This practice cultivates a positive atmosphere and reinforces their commitment to one another.

Reflection prompts and future planning activities not only deepen emotional connections but also encourage accountability in recovery. Couples can create a joint accountability plan, outlining how they will support each other through challenges and setbacks. This plan can include specific strategies for managing stress, handling triggers, and seeking help when needed. By developing this accountability framework, partners ensure they are both invested in each other's recovery journeys and committed to navigating challenges as a united front.

Integrating mindfulness practices into their daily routines can further enhance the effectiveness of reflection and planning. Couples can engage in mindfulness exercises together, such as meditation or yoga, to cultivate awareness and presence in their relationship. These practices foster emotional regulation, reduce stress, and improve communication, creating a solid foundation for their partnership.

Ultimately, practical tools like reflection prompts and future planning activities empower couples to actively participate in their recovery journeys. By fostering open communication, emotional intimacy, and shared aspirations, these tools enhance the overall strength of the relationship. Partners become allies in each other's growth, creating a fulfilling life together in sobriety. As they navigate the complexities of recovery, these practical tools serve as a reminder of their commitment to one another and the bright future they are building together.

In this chapter, the emphasis on practical tools such as reflection prompts and future planning activities illustrates the importance of intentionality in nurturing a healthy relationship during recovery. Couples are encouraged to engage in open conversations about their individual and shared goals, fostering a deeper understanding of each other's aspirations. By utilizing creative approaches like vision boards and gratitude exercises, partners can cultivate emotional intimacy and reinforce their commitment to supporting one another's growth. The focus on shared experiences and individual pursuits not only strengthens their bond but also empowers both partners to thrive in sobriety. As they navigate their journey together, these practices serve as vital touchpoints, reminding them of their resilience and the rewarding life they are building hand in hand.

Love as a Healing Journey

The journey through this book has covered many facets of navigating recovery together, offering practical insights and guidance for couples committed to a life of sobriety. Beginning with the importance of mutual support and understanding, Chapter 1 laid the groundwork by exploring the significance of establishing trust as the foundation of recovery-focused relationships. This trust set the stage for Chapter 2, which focused on establishing healthy boundaries as each person works on their personal recovery while nurturing the relationship. In Chapter 3, the theme of independence was woven in with a deep respect for each person's individual journey, while Chapter 4 focused on tools to set boundaries effectively, creating an environment that respects both individual and shared needs.

In Chapter 5, the spotlight moved to the unique challenges of relationships in early recovery, where couples learned to build connections on a foundation of mutual growth rather than old, unhealthy patterns. This was extended in Chapter 6, which explored family dynamics and the process of healing old wounds and rebuilding bonds with loved ones. Chapter 7 introduced the importance of surrounding oneself with positive friendships, both new and old, that respect sobriety and encourage a healthy lifestyle. Chapter 8 took the discussion further into the realm of intimacy, offering ways for partners to reconnect both emotionally and physically, emphasizing healthy communication and understanding.

The complex dynamics of dependency and co-dependency were central to Chapter 9, which encouraged the development of interdependence and balance in relationships. Following this, Chapter 10 brought in methods for supporting each other's recovery without crossing into enabling behaviors, reinforcing the importance of encouragement and accountability. Chapter 11 shifted the focus toward creating new memories and traditions that reinforce a sober life, while Chapter 12 addressed the inevitable challenges of life—financial stress, career changes, and more—and how to face them together without falling back on past coping mechanisms.

Chapter 13 explored the spiritual aspects of recovery, encouraging couples to seek a deeper connection and find shared beliefs that can serve as an anchor. Chapter 14 discussed the importance of fostering individual growth alongside the relationship, ensuring that both partners continue to evolve in ways that support both their personal recovery and their partnership. Finally, Chapter 15 provided a look ahead at growing old together in sobriety, underscoring the need for adaptability, resilience, and the enduring commitment to a shared sober life.

Each chapter has offered not just insights but practical tools and exercises, empowering couples to take concrete steps toward a fulfilling and sustainable recovery. As readers move forward, they are reminded of the progress they've made and the strength they've cultivated together. The journey continues with the understanding that recovery, like love, is a commitment renewed each day, a promise to grow together through every season of life.

A relationship grounded in recovery is not just about the commitment to sobriety but about nurturing a continuous path of growth, discovery, and evolution. Each partner's journey in recovery is an individual path, yet a unique blend of self-discovery also occurs when two people grow together, sharing triumphs and setbacks, insights and transformations. Encouraging one another to explore these layers of self offers a chance to deepen the relationship as it matures, allowing it to be a space of exploration as well as support.

A relationship in recovery thrives when both people can openly share their insights and explore new dimensions of themselves. This encouragement goes beyond mere support and transforms into active participation in each other's growth—an interest in discovering together what matters most, what dreams are worth pursuing, and what new habits or hobbies might bring fulfillment. This approach not only strengthens the partnership but also enables each person to redefine who they are beyond addiction or past challenges, allowing the relationship itself to be a safe place for discovery.

Embracing ongoing growth also means nurturing curiosity, both about the world and each other. Over time, couples may find that their shared experiences take on new meanings as perspectives shift and change. New interests, insights, and passions can emerge, revealing sides of each partner that may not have been visible before. These shared discoveries bring freshness to the relationship and reinforce that growth in recovery isn't confined to overcoming addiction—it extends to every part of life.

This mutual encouragement supports a cycle of positive reinforcement, where each partner's progress inspires and uplifts the other. Engaging in new learning experiences together, whether through hobbies, educational pursuits, or even joint therapy sessions, fosters a shared purpose, fueling a sense of unity that strengthens the commitment to sobriety. With each new shared achievement, partners deepen their bond and develop a richer appreciation for each other's journey.

Encouraging one another's growth means creating an atmosphere of acceptance and openness, where each person feels free to pursue personal goals and share those discoveries with their partner. For long-term fulfillment, it is essential to maintain this openness and foster curiosity about the future. Together, couples can continue to build a life that not only supports their sobriety but also allows them to grow into their fullest selves, side by side, through every phase of recovery.

Through Every Season

We began as two, both broken and worn,
With hearts stitched together, both mended and torn.
In shadows we stumbled, in light we grew,
Finding strength not alone, but as one made of two.
Through laughter and heartache, through triumph and pain,
We weathered the storms, we danced in the rain.
We built something sacred, more precious than gold,
A bond that grows deeper as we both grow old.
Hand in hand, we face what tomorrow may bring,
With faith like an anchor, like birds on the wing.
We are healing and whole, forever entwined,
In each other's embrace, we leave the past behind.
So here's to the journey, the love that we share,
To battles and blessings, to hope and to prayer.
Through every new chapter, in joy or in strife,
Together, we're writing a sober life.

Also by Kaitlyn Doht

Renewed Horizons: Embracing Life After Rehab
Pathways to Purpose: Thriving in Transitional Sober Living
Love and Relationships Building Relationships Beyond Addiction